The YOUNGEST ONE in the ROOM

INDIGORIVER
PUBLISHING

The YOUNGEST ONE in the ROOM

DAYNA ADELMAN

The Youngest One in the Room

© 2025 by Dayna Adelman

Library of Congress Control Number: 2024927539
ISBN: 978-1-964686-26-4 (paperback) 978-1-964686-27-1 (ebook)

This book is based on true events reflecting the author's memory of them. Some names and characteristics may have been changed, some events compressed, and some dialogue recreated.

Editors: Marsi Carson, Deborah Froese, Jennie Seitz
Cover and Interior Design: Emma Elzinga

Printed in the United States of America

First Edition

3 West Garden Street, Ste. 718
Pensacola, FL 32502
www.indigoriverpublishing.com

Ordering Information:

Quantity sales: Special discounts are available on quantity purchases by corporations, associations, and others. For details, contact the publisher at the address above.

Orders by US trade bookstores and wholesalers: Please contact the publisher at the address above.

With Indigo River Publishing, you can always expect great books, strong voices, and meaningful messages. Most importantly, you'll always find . . . *words worth reading.*

To Alani Maia, Devyn Skyler, and Perri Brynn:
my smart, silly, adventurous, and overall wonderful nieces.

Your bright eyes, inquisitive minds, and love fill me with inspiration
and energize me about the future.

I can't wait to see what you three become in this world,
what the working environment looks like when you enter the workforce,
and the impact I know you will each make in your own unique ways.

Never stop shining bright and dreaming.

Love, Aunt Day Day

CONTENTS

FOREWORD

We live in an era filled with so much talking. We scroll through social media feeds filled with an overwhelming, paralyzing array of opinions, perspectives, and judgments. But some voices stand out—the ones that are unafraid to take bold, meaningful actions for themselves and the broader communities around them. These are the people who show resilience in the most difficult situations and navigate extreme complexity to achieve their goals. At every turn, they show continuous forward momentum.

Dayna Adelman is one of those people.

I met Dayna in 2010 when she began her career at a public relations agency. Since then, we've worked together at multiple companies in multiple industries, which gave me a front row seat to witness her extraordinary growth. She went from being the most junior person on my team to being the most senior person on my team.

And one day, I'm sure I'll work for her.

Dayna has become one of my closest friends and one of the people I love most in the world. She is instantly likable; she's warm, approachable, and charming, with a silly and self-deprecating sense of humor. She's also smart, ambitious, and brave. It's a powerful cocktail in life and in business.

I nicknamed her Velvet Hammer for her ability to leverage soft skills, emotional intelligence, and an empathetic style while consistently delivering a strong "take no excuses" impact on the business.

In the following pages, you'll learn about her impressive journey. You'll discover her humor when you read about her impromptu appearance on Broadway. You'll be charmed by the Thanksgiving dinner she hosted for twenty Dutch colleagues—despite the fact that she had no clue how to cook a turkey! You'll experience her bravery when she navigated working in a new industry run almost entirely by older men. You'll witness her ambition when she decided to move abroad from the US. And hopefully, you'll see yourself in a story that celebrates taking chances, embracing mistakes, and going after what you want in life.

Tara Rush Tripp

January 2024

INTRODUCTION

My mom calls me Forrest Gump. She calls me that for a specific reason. Over my school and professional years, I have found myself in a myriad of situations that "most people" (by her definition) would not. I have come to realize that most of these situations have been thanks to being in the right place at the right time, coupled with a little bit of skill and a whole lot of luck.

I have also come to not only embrace the descriptor, but to live my life like Forrest Gump. I wouldn't be who I am today without pivotal Forrest Gump moments.

I distinctly remember being selected in fourth grade to play the president of the board of education in a simulation we ran in school. I had no idea what I was doing or what the board of education even was, but I muddled my way through. This was one of my earliest memories of what would become many fake-it-until-you-make-it moments in my life. A long folding table was set up in the auditorium for the event, and I sat at the center of the table, proudly behind the placard that said my name and "President," as I confidently banged the gavel to motion that the meeting had commenced.

When I was around 18, I won day-of lottery tickets for twenty-five dollars to see *The 25th Annual Putnam County Spelling Bee* on Broadway and ended up on stage for ninety minutes as one of the spelling bee participants. The show was new, and word had not yet spread that the production included some participation from the audience. I was separated from my friend in the lobby before the show, given a short briefing, and shown to my seat in the audience, where I anxiously waited for what would come next. Shortly after the opening number, I was brought on stage for my Broadway debut. As the action unfolded around me—the story, the songs—I sat tall on the bleachers on stage, smiling and bopping around like I knew what I was doing or what was going to happen next. I was pulled up to dance at certain points and somehow seamlessly fell into following the guidance of my on-stage attendant. And then it was my turn. As a spelling bee participant, I was called to the microphone to spell my first word. I proudly leaned into the microphone and spelled cow. "C-O-W. Cow." The audience cheered, and my smile went from ear to ear as I was shuffled back to the bleachers and the show progressed. I had just delivered a line—on a Broadway stage—how the heck did this happen?! Just as quickly as it had started, my Broadway debut came to a crashing end when I misspelled some preposterous word I cannot recall now. I was swiftly ushered back to my seat in the audience with an Apple & Eve juice box and a participation pin. I still have these two items on display in my childhood bedroom today.

When I was in my mid-twenties, I was selected by my company to participate in a sustainable impact competition in Amsterdam at a time in my life when I knew little about sustainability. Little did I know, but this opportunity would indelibly change the trajectory of my career. More on that in the pages to come.

Forrest Gump also happens to be one of my favorite movies.

I admire Forrest—his persistence in the face of adversity. His curiosity. And his innate ability to tell a story in his own unique way. He is inspiring without trying to be. His distinct character traits make him who he is and separate him from who he is not.

The movie is an emotional rollercoaster. Sometimes I find myself smiling. Sometimes, laughing. Sometimes, heartbroken and bawling my eyes out. Getting through the two-hour-and-twenty-two-minute film usually requires more than a handful of tissues.

But that's life, is it not? An emotional rollercoaster—sometimes you are on the way up, your heart rate beating fast, waiting for what's to come next. And then, with little to no warning, you're sliding all the way down. Your nerves are bundled in the pit of your stomach, and you're left wondering what is going to happen next or, worse, you're left figuring out what you *want* next.

We've all been there throughout our lives—from the day we learned to walk and talk, we're constantly navigating our own rollercoasters. Just when we think we've successfully completed and stepped off one, there's always another to follow.

The Youngest One in the Room started as a collection of anecdotes and self-reflections from my first decade of working my way through the trials and tribulations of corporate America as a young female. At first, it was a journal meant for my eyes only as I tried to make sense of my career to date during the COVID-19 pandemic while trying to gain clarity on what I wanted out of the next ten years. The idea of turning it into a proper book only came to me as I continued to write, and the lessons learned from navigating the workplace began to give way to a connected storyline chronicling the first decade of my career rather than a collection of disparate stories.

I am a passionate communications professional who started my career at a mid-sized New York City-based communications agency in 2010. This first experience gave me the hands-on learning I needed to build solid roots in the multifaceted world of strategic communications—from brand-building to crisis communications. After almost three years there, I moved on to a large-scale advertising agency where I worked in a truly integrated communications setting, getting a firsthand look at the wonderful world of advertising while still practicing communications. These were the early days in the rise of social and digital media as well, and I had a front row seat as I watched it unfold inside one of New

York's iconic Madison Avenue advertising agency darlings.

I jumped at the opportunity to get into the corporate world when it came knocking in 2014. I joined the US subsidiary of one of the world's largest brewers and haven't looked back. It had always been my goal to live and work abroad after interning in London during my junior year of college, and I saw the opportunity to one day do that with my then new employer.

When I wrote this back in 2021, I had held five different roles with my employer at the time since 2014 and 2020: communications manager supporting both external and internal communications for the US business; director of Corporate Social Responsibility looking after our environmental, social, and responsibility agendas in the US; crisis and issues manager on the global corporate affairs team in Amsterdam; global international brands and cider public relations manager in Amsterdam; and director of External Communications in the United States.

Okay, but really, who am I?

I'm a thirty-something who likes to do things outside the box. I've always had a little extra "pep in my step," especially when it comes to doing things that "nice Jewish girls from Long Island" wouldn't do—from where I went to college to where I work today, spending time living abroad, and everything in between. I broke the mold that typically consisted of spending a few years after college working in New York City, meeting your future husband, marrying said husband, having kids, outgrowing your small apartment, and then moving to the suburbs. I have nothing against the mold, and I adore spending time with my family and friends who did follow what is, for us, a more traditional path in life. It just wasn't for me.

I was the theater kid as much as I was part of the sports crowd, having my hand in a little bit of everything throughout my whole life. My varied interests led me to become adaptable and flexible for whatever situation I may find myself in.

My upbringing undoubtedly shaped me. I experienced a turbulent childhood living with a verbally abusive father, who was finally removed from our home when I was fifteen. Everything I do, I do to show the world that kids like us—the ones who grew up hearing we weren't good enough or wouldn't amount to anything—can succeed. I built a form of resilience in those early days that only later in life could I attribute to these formative years.

I never wanted pity for my situation, but I was driven to succeed in life for many reasons because of it. I wanted to succeed for those who stepped up—my mother and my maternal grandparents. I wanted to succeed because I never wanted to rely on anyone else financially. I wanted to succeed to prove that there are different forms of success, and choosing the unconventional path, as compared to those who grew up around me, can be just as satisfying. At the end of the day, I believe you have to do what is right and best for you, not what society around you expects. So that is what I did, and what I continue to do.

Family is extremely important to me. I am very close to my mother and sister and mourn the loss of my beloved maternal grandparents each and every day. I am a proud aunt to three beautiful nieces, Alani Maia, age seven (although she will tell you "seven and three-fourths"), Devyn Skyler, age three, and Perri Brynn, who, by far, has the coolest birthday, born on March 21, 2023 (3-2-1-2-3!). While I don't live close by, I try to spend as much time with them as possible, whether that be through long weekend visits or FaceTime video calls.

It would take a few years for me to figure out how to give my family my undivided attention, specifically how to leave work at work or reprioritize other catch-up calls with friends when I am playing with them. But now when I am with them, the emails stop and the replies to SMS and WhatsApp messages just have to wait. To me, there truly is nothing more important than pushing my nieces on swings; losing time and time again to a kindergartener in a game of Trouble or the unicorn version of Monopoly or chess (*yes*, chess); schooling my mom, sister, and brother-in-law in a game of Rummikub; or reading the girls a bedtime story while clutching the stuffed version of the character from the book tightly. I have, however, managed to dodge changing diapers, feeding bottles of formula, and giving baths—three things I don't have patience or the stomach for. Have you smelled a bottle of formula?!

I am an avid traveler who finds inspiration from exploring. I love to experience new people, places, and cultures. I jump at the chance to go on any adventure—big or small. And I absolutely love food! I'd rather have an incredible meal complimented with a stellar wine than buy a new pair of shoes (but I also really like shoes and always find a way to buy them too).

I'm a reader and a writer. I adore going to the theater, and I also love to be on stage. I thoroughly enjoy telling a good story and making people laugh, and sometimes, when merited, cry. I've been a maid of honor three times, so I think it is safe to say I am a good friend. I absolutely love that I have friends all over the country and the world.

The purpose of writing was to tell my story and what I learned from it while giving you, the reader, the freedom to take what you need from it. Too many career-related books tell us what we *should* do with our careers. A career—in any profession—for men and women—is not a one-size-fits-all experience. It's a journey of self-discovery. Therefore, I hope that you walk away feeling inspired to go on your *own* journey—whether that be at the onset of a career, the middle, or even the end.

And while I do believe I am like Forrest Gump, I also believe that I am not the only one—rather, there is a little Forrest in all of us. After all, none of us knows what life has in store until we dive in and sample it—just like Forrest's famous box of chocolates.

PART 1

A JOURNEY BEGINS

Chapter 1

CHOCOLATE

A box of chocolate. A great, gooey pool of opportunity.

What? Is that not the way *you* look at chocolate?

In life, there are tons of opportunities. I think it is just a matter of being able to recognize and seize them. Which, don't get me wrong, is usually *very* tough to do.

I am grateful for all the opportunities I've been afforded thus far in this life, particularly my first professional experience. More on that shortly.

At a young age, I realized opportunities weren't just granted. They had to be earned. In the third grade, I overheard a conversation that changed my life. I was a gregarious kid. My friends and I were into everything. We played multiple sports. We danced. We took acting classes and art classes, and this class and that. And we drove our parents nuts with the boundless energy we exhibited running through their houses and yards. My sister, on the other hand, was different. Quieter and more serious; studious from a young age. Whereas I would tire myself out by day's end and put myself to bed before it was time, she would stay up until all hours of the night reading under the covers with a flashlight. I like to think we balanced each other out. Two of me at that young age would've been a lot!

One day in the third grade, when my class was in between classroom time and a specialty activity, I overheard two teachers comparing me to my sister. Maybe because I was a child of a teacher and knew teachers talked about their students, or maybe because I was acutely observant even at a young age, I heard my name, heard the comment about how rowdy I was compared to my sister ("So completely opposite, those two"), and took the sting to heart for many years.

At the tender age of nine, what I hadn't learned yet was that being different—or, in this case, *"opposite"*—was okay. However, I did learn something important that day—I learned self-awareness. I wouldn't be able to name what I had learned until years later, but I somehow figured out, from that moment on, how to temper myself in different situations. I saved the energy for the playgrounds and fields, and I found my "inside voice" in school.

I can't claim I ever worked *as* hard and became *as* studious as my sister, but I learned how to play the politics game. I learned how to gain trust and respect in the classroom, which was different from what it takes to gain the trust of a coach on the field or a director on the stage. I worked hard to balance this newfound skill, and it wasn't until years later that I reflected on how it paid off. What appeared to my mom as "Forrest Gump" moments were hard-earned opportunities realized in some unique and interesting ways.

One year after "the teacher incident," when I was selected from all my classmates in the same grade to play the president of the board in the mock simulation, the unit was meant to teach us about the importance of the board and what their role was in running our schools. I took the role seriously—dressing in my best version of fourth-grade business casual with a blazer and skirt, making sure I spoke clearly and projected, and finding a way to sound authoritative on a topic I knew nothing about. Later that year, my teacher selected me to represent our class and speak on the topic of "Fourth-Grade Memories" at our elementary school graduation ceremony. I remember the multicolored dress I wore that was a mix of some of my favorite colors—lavender, turquoise, and navy—with flowers on the bottom, as I spoke about the different units we experienced that year, from Long Island geography to science, and where we took our class trips. I am almost certain my speech included a memory about the time our substitute teacher's chinchillas made a visit to our class. He was covering for our teacher, who was on maternity leave, and introduced us to the furry rodents. I can still picture the elaborate cage that served as their home, equipped with multicolored tunnels that looked like a fun park for small creatures. A great memory for my peers, and a nightmare of an image for our parents because we all came home begging for our own furry friends.

By fifth grade, I had garnered the confidence to run for class president of the Student Council. I ran on the platform "Pickles for All."

What is *that* you may ask?

I was not satisfied with the small, circular, ridged pickles that were served alongside the deli sandwiches (only two-to-three of them per person!) in the cafeteria. I wanted the big, full-size New York deli pickles. We students deserved that, after all!

I won the election that year, and every middle school student council election after that. I was never able to deliver on the fifth-grade pickle promise, but I did work hard. I put in loads of after-school hours and worked on anti-bullying campaigns as part of a peer leadership group. I also woke up early every Friday morning for four years to run the Friday morning bagel sale. The winters were especially tough—it was so dark and cold—but we had to be ready for the students who would rush through the main entrance doors hungry and raring to eat a fresh New York bagel every Friday. All of this was done in service of making the school a better place.

These were things I did because I liked to do them. No one told me I had to. No one told me what I'd learn from doing so. I liked people. These interactions gave me energy. I learned that I liked talking to people—all kinds of people. In fact, I liked speaking to crowds a lot!

In my later middle school and high school years, I leaned into this. I took my love for acting more seriously by taking classes on Long

Island and in New York City, and I was always in the school chorus. I even attended a select summer singing program with two classmates and kids from across New York City and Long Island, who trained and prepared us to join a professional adult choir for a grand performance. One summer it was a production of "Carmina Burana." We performed on the beautiful Tilles Center stage on Long Island, and after, I got to meet the then-US senator from Massachusetts, John Kerry, who was in the audience!

In eighth grade I was in a performance of *Pippin* at a local theater company. It was a young people's theater edition. I was privileged to get to perform consistently amongst some of the most talented kids in the New York City area, most of whom were one-to-five years older than me. As we performed "Morning Glow" to end Act 1, I remember singing my heart out and raising my arms toward my peer playing the character Pippin in tandem with all the others as per the choreography. I looked out at the blur of the audience and thought, *This is incredible. This is the best high I've ever felt*, which was later on accompanied by another internal thought: *Why would people do drugs when they can just do musical theater?!*

My *"Pippin"* moment is one I often come back to. I am always trying to emulate that specific high that happens in those climactic moments on stage when the intensity in music meets the intensity in plot, leaving the audience and the performer wanting more. While this exact moment could never be recreated, it could, of course, be found in other ways.

These years were crucial in building and shaping me. It taught me discipline—I had to be at rehearsal on time, which meant I needed to have studied and done my homework beforehand. It taught me respect and gratitude—I had to rely on my mom for transportation on nights and weekends to rehearsals, and only because she agreed to shuttle me around could I partake. It taught me resourcefulness—how to create a costume with items that already existed in my closet (or my mom's or sister's), so I didn't have to ask my mom for money. And it taught me the value of teamwork and commitment—how you can work together to create an ensemble that, in turn, creates something so beautiful and powerful—and is bigger than any one individual.

On paper, it was a beautiful childhood, but I also made it a beautiful childhood by keeping busy—running from activity to activity seven days a week and staying out of the house—because it wasn't always rainbows and butterflies.

Another thing I didn't realize until years later: I was working intently to build a thick, resilient skin in my middle and early high school years. I was the girl who'd get callbacks for theatrical roles but mostly end up in the ensemble. I took it on the chin. I used those experiences to hone my acting skills. To this day, I joke with some friends that there wouldn't have been "X show" without Dayna Adelman holding up the ensemble! And I think I became a far better performer because of it—where else can you go from playing a hooker on the streets of London in *Jekyll and Hyde* in October to a bar patron in France cheering on the "Master of the House" in *Les Misérables* in December while simultaneously playing an orphan in *Annie* in the same month?!

When I was around fourteen and in my last year of middle school, my soccer team broke up, and there were tryouts for the team that played at one level up from us (Travel A team). Most of my peers from our now defunct Travel B team made it, and I did not. I was upset. Really upset. All my friends were now on the A team! Maybe I wasn't as good, but I wanted to be there so badly.

Another coach—the one who coached a group of girls a year older than me—got wind of this and asked me to try out with his team for the season. I did, albeit a bit reluctantly. I was still in middle school, and these girls were in high school. On top of that, most of them had grown up in a different part of town than me, so I didn't know them from previous years at school. I felt super intimidated at the tryout, but I made the team. And not only that, I made several really good friends—one who is still a dear friend to this day.

These formative years came with a lot of reward but also a lot of hard work. From early before-school commitments to making it through the school day only then to balance sports practice with acting lessons and rehearsals at night, I was constantly living a complicated balancing act. Running on all that youthful energy, I found a way to stay committed. I learned the true meaning of dedication. Quitting was never an option for me, although I think my mom would've appreciated having fewer places to pick me up *and* drop me off at odd hours during the week and on the weekends. I am forever indebted to what she sacrificed in her own life to make mine a reality. These days, when I ask her if she regrets allowing me to do everything, it is always a clear, "No! I absolutely loved those years, especially the shows. I loved the friends you made. It was our community." She says this with a smile. But she's always quick to add, "Although I definitely could've done without the late-night rehearsal pick-ups or the cold pre-winter New York days on the soccer field," with a laugh to suggest she's only joking.

The active life I pursued outside of home also kept me away from what was brewing at home. My father's narcissism would only grow over this time period. His fits of verbal rage would be more frequent. He was an amazing success, and everyone else a failure. His way was the best, and the door was always there for others who didn't agree to leave. Over the phone, he filled his parents' ears—the only ears that would listen—with how great he was, how wonderful his business was, and what everyone else was doing wrong during late-night, midweek conversations that reverberated off the high living room ceilings and traveled upstairs to our bedrooms where we tried to sleep. His mother always sided with her son, and my sister and I lost contact with her when I was around the age of fourteen.

My mother was easing out of being a stay-at-home mother, so she was at work some of the time. My father started traveling a lot more for work. When he was home, the tension was thick with nasty words spewing from his mouth. He tried to pull us apart, but he failed miserably. His actions brought us closer together. A strong, unbreakable bond was built between my mother, sister, and me—one that still exists today.

I vowed to be everything he was not. Whereas I was an opportunity seeker, he was an opportunity denier. He had every chance to be a part of my life, but he chose himself over me, my sister, and my mother.

When my mom was working on a Saturday, he was tasked with taking me to soccer. Oftentimes, he'd tell me right before the game that he was too busy and that I'd have to find a ride. One time, he pulled this stunt early on a Saturday morning. Mortified that it was happening again, I picked up the landline and sheepishly dialed my friend who lived up the block. She quickly asked her parents if they could take me with them. They said it was no problem, but they were going for lunch right before soccer, so they'd pick me up early and I could go for lunch with them.

When we sat down for lunch, the family started showering my friend's mother with gifts. It was her birthday. I, of course, had no clue. Here I was, eleven years old in my sleek, black-and-white soccer uniform, sitting at their family table on a spring day with friends I've known my whole life. It should have been great, right? But I wanted nothing more than for the bench I was sitting on to open up and swallow me alive. I choked back tears and muscled a smile so I could join the chorus of "Happy Birthday to you . . ." After all, it was the least I could do for these people who had once again shown up for me when my own father could not.

My father would never accept help. His way was best. It was his castle, and we were all just living there. If something set him off, even the simplest things—like my sister doing her homework at the kitchen counter where he wanted to work or my mom asking him to do something—he'd again point to the door and suggest that my mom, sister, and I leave.

Our situation at home could have filled me with so much anger and rage, and—to be fair—sometimes I let it. Similar to the change I made after my third-grade teacher's offhand comment, I made a vow shortly after crashing the birthday lunch that I was going to rise above it. I was going to work hard. I was going to succeed. I was going to take advantage of any opportunities that came. I was going to be independent and financially stable when I was older. I didn't want to rely on anyone financially, especially not a man. And one day, I was going to be able to take care of my mom the way she managed to take care of my sister and me. Even in those darkest of days at home, there was still a bright light. There was always a "box of chocolates."

Sometimes you bite into a piece and want to spit it out right away, but when you find the ones that you've been looking for, you learn to hold on and savor them, eternally etch them in your mind.

Admittedly, this isn't something I learned on my own. This was an important lesson my mother taught me. I can vividly remember her whispering this simple, yet sage, advice in my ear dozens of times over the years: when coming off the stage with a full face of makeup after a performance; right after my giving a speech in front of all my peers; and hugging me tight as we stood along the Seine on my seventeenth birthday, watching the lights twinkle atop the Eiffel Tower as we visited my sister who was studying in Paris.

"Remember this moment forever," she said. And I did. I always do.

As I learned at a young age, those are the moments—the energizing moments—that you will revisit over and over in your life.

Chapter 2

THE START OF A PROFESSIONAL JOURNEY

I graduated from the University of North Carolina (UNC) at Chapel Hill in May 2010 with bachelor's degrees in journalism and mass communication (with a specialty in PR) and dramatic arts. I am equally proud of both degrees and can confidently say I use both every single day. I absolutely love the Carolina Tar Heels, especially the basketball team and Coach Roy Williams, which means I despise our decades-old Tobacco Road rival, Duke, and Coach Mike Krzyzewski.

In my senior year, I felt the pressure—like most other graduating seniors—to land a job before the end of the term. My sister graduated three years earlier from the same university with a degree in business administration. I vividly remembered watching her go through the process—lots of interviews that happened in mid-October of her senior year with offers made by the end of that first semester. She set the precedent for our family: you go to a good school, you get a good job. And I wanted that more than anything. But the world of communications—more specifically, public relations or corporate communications—was different. Hiring is done on an as-needed basis versus the financial institutions and management consulting firms who have an entry-level class they fill each year. I knew what I wanted: a job at one of the top PR firms in New York. At least, that is what I *thought* I wanted. But landing it months in advance of graduation was proving to be an impossible feat.

I was entering the workforce in one of the worst recessions in years. We watched Wall Street giants, such as Lehman Brothers, fall before our eyes. Jobs in any sector were few and far between. I didn't know anyone who landed a real job from the class of 2009 at a PR firm—they were all interns who were now snatching up the entry-level, full-time jobs one year later.

I not only had the pressure that I put on myself, but also the family expectation that I would come out of school with a degree *and* a job. I remember explaining endlessly that in my field, there was no such thing as a guaranteed job before Christmas, let alone spring break, or even graduation. Every conversation seemed to go around and around, something like this:

"Anything new with the job search?" my mom would ask caringly.

Insert flare-up in the pit of the stomach and cue the anxiety.

"No," I would repeat. "As I said, communications doesn't work like finance or banking. No one is recruiting now for roles that will be open in June. Plus, everyone who graduated last year is *still* looking for jobs. I am going to apply for internship applications when they open in January/February."

"Okay, great. I know you're trying," she'd reply.

I panicked. I started to look at other options and tried to convince myself there was a different path out there. In fact, I applied for, and was accepted into, the prestigious Teach for America program, a part of the AmeriCorps national service network. It is an amazing program for which I have the utmost respect, but as I got closer to graduation, the reality of the job sunk in. I have nothing but admiration for teachers, but I also wasn't fooling anyone—I had no desire to be a teacher. I don't really like kids (who I am not related to), and I don't have a ton of patience. I imagined myself standing in front of a classroom of high school seniors in Washington, DC, where I was placed—me staring at them, them staring at me. In this image, I was paralyzed. Maybe a blink here and there. Maybe.

This seemed like a recipe for disaster. I decided to back out of the program, giving them enough time to fill my spot with someone deserving, who wanted it more than I did. To this day, I wonder what it would've been like, but I do not regret my decision.

Instead, I began to focus on applying for internships at a handful of the big PR agencies in NYC at the time—Ketchum, Ogilvy, MSL—and I got some! I was also enjoying the interview process. Some of them included in-person challenge days where you took tests, met with employees for interviews, and networked directly with your peers who were potential colleagues—but also your competition. A bit Machiavellian, I suppose, but also a good foundation for what it's like in the real world.

So, that became my plan. My plan A. Spend the summer doing an internship, see if I even liked working in this field, see if it goes anywhere, and then reevaluate. If it doesn't work out, plan B would be to take some time to try my hand at auditioning—give that a whirl. What a plan! By mid-April, I was set, and I was happy. And then an opportunity came along . . .

❖

In March 2010, I had a chat with the career advisor within the journalism school at UNC. He wanted to connect me with an alum who was based in New York City and worked at a midsize PR agency that I had never heard of.

We were now at the height of the worldwide social media boom. Facebook had recently opened up to users beyond American university students and even the general American population. The world was now on Facebook. Twitter was becoming a thing, and smartphones were rapidly on the rise. Well, BlackBerries were fast on the rise—no one could really afford an iPhone at the time.

I decided to put my newfound social media skills to work and looked up this alum a few days later. And wow—she was impressive. Recently named one of PR Week's "30 Under 30s"; and the agency she worked for had just won PR Week's "Midsize Agency of the Year" *and* overall "Agency of the Year." Not bad. It was a sister agency to one of the biggest PR agencies within the Omnicom Network and had several high-profile clients. Naturally, I wanted to reach out.

So, I did and . . . *nothing happened.* No response.

I am sure you're expecting me to say I was heartbroken, but I wasn't. Because I was stubborn and naive. To use a quote from my favorite nineties sitcom, I thought, *How rude!* and moved on. I decided in that moment to stay the course with my internship applications and my plan A.

About a month later in early April, I was heading up to New York for some of the internship interviews, and that (often pesky) internal voice told me to reach out to that alum again. It was the voice of persistence. So I reached out. This time, I got a response! I received a really nice apology for the delay. In the time since I had originally emailed (late February/early March), in addition to being busy winning impressive awards, this person had moved across the country to help grow the Los Angeles office for the agency. She was managing a full line of business with a major banking client during the foreclosure crisis and the "great recession."

I learned an important first lesson here: People are *busy!* People in all fields are busy. People in PR are *always* busy. They barely have time to do the things they even *want* to do. Why would they take the time to talk to you? But then again, if you never reach out, you'll never know. Finding the balance between persistence and being annoying is hard. It's a fine line, but it is doable. Something else I've come to learn in time.

My NYC contact, now my LA contact, graciously set me up with some informational interviews with two of her colleagues in NYC. I remember walking into the office nervously and looking around. I expected to see throngs of young people and lots of noise—people on the phone, chatter in the halls, creativity reverberating against the walls.

There were lots of offices and cubicles, but curiously, no people. It was eerily quiet. I mean it when I say you could hear a pin drop. And the office was carpeted. It was . . . weird.

I was ushered into a small vacant office and waited for my first of two chats. I waited. And waited. And waited. I didn't have a smartphone at the time, so I read my resume and looked at my notes on the company over and over and over. Unsure of what to do—and clearly no one around to ask—I stood up, gazed out at Midtown Manhattan from the window, and waited some more. Finally, after what seemed like an eternity, my interviewer joined me in the room. In reality, it had only been about twenty to thirty minutes.

She apologized, as she was running late from a doctor's appointment. This was also something I did not understand at the time. Why would someone go to the doctor during the workday? Ah, the innocence of the non-working youth. Well, duh, Dayna, if people work nine-to-five-plus during the week, and most doctor's offices are closed on nights and weekends, when are people supposed to go to the doctor? It was one of the first wake-up calls that the days of endless winter and summer breaks were soon to be a thing of the past.

Overall, the conversation was informative and went well, and I was passed along to the next person. In this conversation, I think we spent more time talking about my acting degree (and hobby) than we did about communications and PR, which was fine since this was more of a get-to-know-you conversation. However, it was a microlesson in how to—or how not to—steer a conversation during an interview or otherwise. You live and you learn, right?

After about an hour and thirty minutes total, it was time to go. I left the same way I had come. Back through the people-less corridors.

Somewhat confused by the overall experience, I followed up to thank each interviewer for his and her time, and to thank my LA connection for setting up the conversations. Although hesitant, I expressed interest in continuing the conversation. I was somewhat intrigued, and the curiosity burning inside me just had to find out where everyone was that day. A conference? An office outing to help the community? A very, very early happy hour?

A few days later, I received a call back. Apparently, I had made some sort of an impression, and the company wanted to set up a series of phone interviews with some senior members of the team. I remember preparing for these conversations by—once again—applying my newfound social and digital media research skills. As LinkedIn was not so widely used at this time, I turned my attention to reviewing every nook and cranny of the company website and completely lucked out. The great thing about this agency back in those days was that each employee had a quirky photo and answers to one or two absurd questions standing in as a bio. I remember thinking, *What pose would I strike in my picture and what would I say my favorite ice cream flavor is if I were to get a job here?*

Looking back on this moment, I realize if you start to envision how you would want to tell prospective and current clients what your favorite ice cream flavor is on a company website, take it as a good sign that you have developed some sort of fondness for the company.

You spend a lot of time at work—in some cases, more time there with your colleagues than you do at home with your family and friends. It is sad, but true. Therefore, the company culture is extremely important. One of my mentors has shared the popular Peter Drucker quote over the years, "Culture eats strategy for breakfast."

Between the first meetings and the phone interviews, I received the exciting news that I had been offered two of the internships I applied for, both at very prestigious NYC firms! I was ecstatic. Everything was falling into place. I graciously accepted one of the offers but was already in the throes of interviews for the full-time position at this firm. I decided to forge ahead with the interviews to see how this would all shake out.

The next series of phone interviews was great. Except for this one woman who kept saying my name incorrectly:

"Hi Dane-YAH. It's very nice to meet you. Could you tell me a little more about yourself?" the lady said on the other end of the line. She seemed warm, from her tone of voice, but I didn't notice it at the time because all I heard was "Dane-YAH."

WHO is Dane-YAH?!

I held my red Motorola flip phone away from my ear to bite down on my lower lip as I cringed. It took every fiber of my being to hold back from shouting, "It is D-A-Y-n-a" into the other end of the phone. In retrospect, I should have said something. It's not like I was trying to school her in her own craft by correcting her. It was my name, after all. *My* name. A quick, "It's actually Dayna, but I get that all the time," would've done the trick. But I didn't do that. I didn't have the guts. I didn't want to risk throwing the tone of the interview off or appearing rude or disrespectful. In short, I didn't stand up for myself, and although the call went well, I didn't feel great about myself after.

It was not long after the Dane-YAH conversation before the call came in with an actual offer.

I GOT A JOB OFFER! I was ecstatic. I felt wanted. I felt smart. I felt empowered. I felt ready to take on my career in the Big, Bad Apple. And my time would come when I had the opportunity to correct the Dane-YAH offender, who just happens to be someone who I greatly admire, and who I am fortunate to have worked for and learned from. In fact, it became a running joke amongst us as well as others who were told the story within due course. I would never live it down, but that was okay. Lesson learned!

When the offer came in, there was only one problem: I was already committed to the internship, which I was also excited about. I had grown to really, really like my plan A. What to do, what to do?

At first, I kept the conversation in my head. I made a pros and cons list *in my own head*. I had the conversation about what I wanted to do *in my own head*. Everything was stuck *in my own head*, and I was driving myself nuts. Eventually I came to realize I needed to get *out of my own head*. I started talking to peers, to former professors, and to family. They all helped provide perspective, but sometimes their perspectives were opposing, and I again found myself conflicted.

I remember that my grandfather, whom we called Papa, was in

favor of my sticking with the internship. After all, it was with a firm he had heard of. He thought that was a safe route to go, whereas my peers pushed me to go for the job. As the patriarch of the family and the man I most admired, I highly respected his opinion, but his advice seemed a bit outdated.

What I realize now that I didn't back then is that when making big decisions such as a first career choice, or any career move for that matter, at the end of the day, the ultimate decision lies with *you*. However, staying in your own head can become maddening. It takes a combination of listening to your gut, seeking opinions from those you trust, and internalizing all the factors. You can never make a decision like this in a day. It's always best to sleep on it—sometimes for a few nights. After a few days of torturing myself, the light was clear. I wanted this job.

After all, I had already selected my response to the ice cream question for the company website: "It's an undecipherable tie between a scoop of homemade mint chocolate chip (green only) and a scoop of homemade rocky road, which leaves the only choice of getting two scoops and putting both in a homemade waffle cone, if available."

I walked in on day one to find an office buzzing with life. Chatter in the halls, lively phone conversations, and colorful charts on the walls from creative brainstorms.

I later came to find out that the NY staff were all in the large conference room holding a funeral for the beloved office pets—two frogs—on the day I came in for the informational interviews. Apparently, one escaped its cozy water world and was unable to live without its mate; the other took the plunge as well. We all know what happens to a fish—or a frog out of water. The lovebirds didn't last long after their escape, and the group decided to honor them with a full funeral service equipped with eulogies. It was absolutely absurd and ridiculous.

I instantly knew I had made the right choice—it's that elated feeling you get when blindly selecting the chocolate from the box that has *the* filling. You know, exactly the one you were after. For me, it was like reaching for and biting into the caramel. I instantly knew I was home.

Chapter 3

THE YOUNGEST ONE IN THE ROOM: THE FIRST ENCOUNTER

June 1, 2010, came faster than I ever could have imagined. I had the month of May to enjoy the graduation festivities, pack up my car, and make the twelve-hour trek from North Carolina to New York one last time. Although I was sad to leave the beauty of Chapel Hill and my college-era lifelong friends behind, I was ready for what lay ahead in NYC.

After a nerve-stricken Memorial Day weekend, as my friends headed to the beach, I headed to 711 Third Avenue from my sister's apartment. At the time, my sister was a management consultant and typically on the road Monday to Thursday, which left her bedroom in her NYC apartment vacant and therefore mine for the taking. This meant I could save some money from my first months of working and not have to do the full commute every day from Long Island, where my mom lived (and technically, so did I). My sister was not a fan of this plan:

"You'll only stay here for emergencies or if you're working late, right?" she clarified.

"Right. I imagine I'll be working late from time to time, and to shlep back to Long Island late at night only to come back the next day is not ideal. Makes so much more sense to just get a good night's sleep, right?" I replied with my fingers crossed behind my back.

"Sure, right."

I told her I'd only do it occasionally when I had to work late nights, but I fully planned on living there Monday to Thursday each week. In fact, I remember moving in not only my clothes, but my food as well. Just enough for that week, of course, so she wouldn't know.

On that very first day I was excited, nervous, overwhelmed. I couldn't help but think, *Today is the first day of the rest of my life!*

That first day whizzed by, but the sights and sounds of my surroundings are still with me: from the stench of New York City trash on a hot day that followed me along my commute to the stomachache that remained with me through the elevator ride up. I keenly remember the introductory meetings and lunch I was treated to outside the office with the team. I am not sure when the nerves quit on that first day.

I tried to soak up everything like a sponge, but truthfully, instructions went in one ear and out the other: so many things to remember, lots of upcoming projects on my accounts. How would I *ever* know what to do? I enjoyed the buzz of chatter around me, although I found it somewhat intimidating as I settled into my cubicle. I was told how to log in to my desktop—no laptops or company phones for junior staff back then! At the time, it didn't even cross my mind that I was nowhere near any windows, and the florescent lighting above me would be my replacement for daylight in the days and weeks to come.

Everything was a blur, but I can confidently recall two things very clearly about that day. First, I was told that I'd be working on three accounts: a cruise line, a national office supply chain store, and a bank. Wait, *what?* Previously I had been told I was working on the cruise line and an office supply store. What's this about a bank? And more specifically, the home loans team? I am twenty-two years old. I am a renter in New York (or not even yet, since I am squatting in my sister's apartment). I do not know anything about mortgages or loan interest rates—how they work or how one obtains one. Numbers and percentages absolutely terrify me. How was I supposed to be of any use on a topic

I knew nothing about?

One of the beauties of this company was that they did not have siloed practice groups. That meant that they didn't have a subset of people just working on travel clients, or corporate clients, or healthcare/pharma clients. It meant that for one portion of your day, you could be working on the upcoming launch of a luxurious floating city and spend the second part of the day creating communication strategies for a bank to reach and inform clients who have found themselves in foreclosure. At the time, of course, it was hard to appreciate this. Now I think this is the best environment to start a career.

So here I was, half excited to launch new cruise ships and half scared to death about figuring out creative ways for a bank to communicate important financial information to their clients who are about to lose their homes. A winning combination, as it turns out! You need the excitement of what you enjoy on the surface to keep you going day to day, and you need to be challenged to be learning and growing. I have since learned to jump at the opportunities that scare me the most, because these are the ones that will challenge me.

The second thing I can tell you about that day was that our most senior client from the bank would be in town, and he requested to meet the *full* team. That included me. In those days, we hadn't yet fully migrated to what I call business casual (good quality jeans every day and a smart-looking top), but it also wasn't super formal. However, for this meeting, I was told business dress was required. Hello, Forrest Gump moment. Debatable if this was about to be a Forrest-in-Vietnam or Forrest-on-shrimp-boat moment, but time would tell.

I was unaware at the time that I was experiencing what I would later coin one of my "youngest one in the room" moments. A phenomenon that I would continue to encounter several times over the years. These are the moments when I steal a beat to look around the room and notice who is there. In the first decade of my career, I had many of these moments when I was, by far, the youngest one present in the meeting. Often it was the youngest, sometimes the only female, the only American, the only this, or the only that.

At first I didn't know what to make of these moments and was left wondering, *Why me?* or *How did I get here?* These moments, especially when young in your career, can be the breeding ground for insecurity and imposter syndrome, but they can equally become moments of pride, confidence-building, learning, and growth. It truly depends on how you take control of the situation and what you make of it.

Taking control of these situations is something I would go on to lean into over the first ten years of my career—sometimes it would work in my favor and sometimes against. Sometimes it was natural to find my voice in the room, sometimes it was harder. But one thing was consistent: I always had an appreciation for being there.

When I recall my first ever "youngest one in the room" moment, before I even knew what a "youngest one in the room" moment was, and before I even got into the room, it started with one small problem.

Because of my underground living situation, the plan was to pack only what I needed—one work outfit per day—in my bag for the week. To my dismay, this meant no options or deviation from the plan unless I wanted to wear my Wednesday outfit on Tuesday and my Tuesday outfit on Wednesday. Before the first day, my mom and I did a little back-to-work shopping, stocking up on the basics I thought I'd need like dresses and skirts for the summer, some colorful patterned or floral tops, black slacks, cardigans in an array of colors, and new flat and heeled shoes. J. Crew, Ann Taylor, Loft, and Banana Republic were my new best friends. In the mix, there were no suits, no pencil skirts, and definitely no restrictive button-down shirts. I hated those! Therefore, this left me in a bit of a conundrum, as I didn't have the proper clothes for this meeting.

Why I did not think to go shopping—as I was in the middle of New York City—I cannot recall. It was probably due to my lack of funds, having just come off being a student the week before, and spending only one day in the working world with no paycheck to my name.

So, there I was, commandeering my sister's room while she was working on a project in California or Minneapolis or Paris, staring at her floor-to-ceiling-length closets that ran along her wall. My sister is five foot ten and very skinny. I am five foot three on a good day and . . . average. This was another problem. I decided to do what any other desperate sister would do. I proceeded to try on *every single* potential item of clothing in the closet. What other choice did I have?

I finally found something that half fit. The blazer sleeves were too long and the pale pink short-sleeve button-down shirt with puff sleeves to go under it was a little tight around my arms, but it would simply have to do.

What did I learn here? Always have a backup! If I'm traveling for business or find myself in a strange or unsettling living situation, I now have a backup in my bag. This pertains to clothing, and *especially* to shoes. Sure, high heels look nice, and open-toe wedge sandals during summer may complement your outfit, but you never know when you're going to need to stand on those feet for longer than anticipated or, unbeknownst to you, view a construction site or brewery that requires socks and closed-toed shoes.

Anyway, here I was on June 2, uncomfortable but at the office and ready for the day. It was an unusually hot day for early June, with temperatures in the high eighties, and what I can only remember feeling like 100 percent humidity. It felt like August in NYC. Our meeting was set to take place after lunch, so I had a few hours to cool down from the morning commute before it began—or so I thought.

With our office supply client, we were preparing our communications plan to support their back-to-school campaign already. The rest of this account team was based in LA, and we needed to pick up some products that would be featured in the client's back-to-school brochure—such as colorful pencil cases, shiny binders, mechanical pencils, and four-pocket folders—from the store to ship out to a reporter ASAP. Not only was I the most junior person on the team—so this task belonged to me—I was also the only one able to jump on it first thing in the morning due to the time difference, with me located in New York and the rest of the team in Los Angeles.

At the time, the closest store to the office was around Forty-Second Street in Times Square. I was on Forty-Fourth and Third Avenue. About a twenty-minute walk from the office across town. No sweat, I thought. Literally. I'll walk. I love to walk.

Forgetting how brutally hot it was, I was soon reminded of the intense heat a few steps into my walk. Too late to turn back, and too poor to jump in a cab, I continued my quest, sweat and all. I also forgot it was summer matinee day for the Broadway shows on Wednesday afternoon, so I was quite literally elbowing my way through a very bustling Times Square.

I got to the store only to learn that the item was out of stock but I could find it at a location further downtown. I looked at my watch, and I knew I needed to be back in the office within an hour for that important client meeting. Without a smartphone, I didn't have access to email, and I also didn't have any of my teammates' phone numbers. What to do? I decided to hop on the subway, grab the item, and beeline it back to the office, confident I could make it in time for the meeting. A daring risk in NYC traffic, and I was clearly not thinking about how hot the subway would be in the extreme heat.

Another key learning opportunity for me was to get someone's phone number on day one! A boss, a peer, a teammate. Would I have wanted to call any of them on day two? No! Absolutely not. But could I if I really needed to? Yes. Except I couldn't. It wasn't an option. I didn't have anyone's number.

With my heart pounding, and my sister's pale pink short puffy-sleeved button-down top that was too tight around my drenched arms, I arrived back in the office just in the nick of time for the meeting. Without a moment to cool down before having to put the blazer on, I jumped into the conference room with the team. Everyone sat down around the oversized and intimidating table. I kept waiting for more team members to file in, but it soon hit me. That was it. And there was one empty chair left for the client. Next to me.

As the client came in, my heart began to beat faster. The sweat came faster too. I smiled, as did everyone around the table. I had no idea what to expect. He had a friendly yet intimidating demeanor. He wanted to start off by going around the room and having everyone introduce themselves before getting down to business. I said a silent prayer, hoping he'd look to his left to begin the around-the-room thing. But no, he looked to his right, directly at me. "Who are you, and what do you do for me?"

My heart was racing, and my stomach was fluttering, reminding me that I hadn't eaten any food up until then. Not much of a breakfast eater on most days, and clearly having to skip lunch due to my office supply store errand, there we were. I had no idea what I said, but I like to think it was something along the lines of "Hi! My name is Dayna Adelman. I am an associate here, and today is my second day, so I look forward to learning more about the business and the team in due course."

Only those in the room with me that day could tell me what I actually said, though I doubt this particular meeting left any lasting impression on them like it did on me. I suppose I will never know. All I know is that I was dressed somewhat appropriately—albeit very sweaty—and I didn't get fired.

It took everything within my power to focus on what the client had to say, not throwing up, and, given the happenings of my last two hours, not passing out.

During that hour or so, I stole a moment to look around the table at my new colleagues. My stomach fluttered again but for a different reason. It hit me right there for the very first time that I was, by far, the youngest one in the room. I pushed the anxiety aside just for a moment to take it all in. It was a momentous instant filled with exhilaration due to both fear and excitement of what was to come.

From that day forward, I started to notice when I was the youngest one in the room. Over a decade later, it still happens quite often, and I think back to that moment fondly, and how much I've learned since then.

They say having a seat at the table is an earned opportunity, but sometimes, such as in this case, it was happenstance.

This is one instance where I learned to "listen louder than you speak." To me, this doesn't mean that you don't speak at all, but that intentional listening usually tops all. I often find that people speak because they want to be perceived as adding value. In other words, they want to validate why they are there. In reality, most people have very little to add, and it is abundantly clear when they are speaking just to be heard. By listening, even if you go into the meeting with nothing prepared to say, you are more likely to pick up on something to add that is valuable.

That said, I also learned to always be prepared. As the youngest person in the room, I have often found those of older generations to be fascinated by the views of the then-mysterious and troubling millennials—particularly when I was early in my career. If asked for your "youngest person" opinion, you need to be prepared to give it. This is another reason why listening can do you good. If you zone out and miss a part of the conversation, you might find yourself caught off guard if asked to actively contribute.

There is power in identifying why you are in a specific room. There's always a reason why you were invited. The reason may not always be evident, so in those cases, I always try to figure out why and use it constructively. Maybe it is to learn something that will help me do my job better, or it is the missing puzzle piece that makes the lightbulb go off for a new idea.

Coupled with this, the process of reflection is something I have started enacting recently. After I figure out why I was invited, prepare for it, and make it through the meeting, I then usually ask myself the following questions: "What did I hear?" "What did I learn?" "How can I apply it?"

I find that going through the above exercises also helps me gain the confidence to speak up. It might sound counterintuitive to "listen louder than you speak," but it is not. I truly believe if you have something to say, by all means, say it. I've learned that people want to hear your opinions or what you surmise from the conversation. This goes back to why you are even there to begin with.

And last, but certainly not least, I learned to read the room. This is a skill that comes in handy on a daily basis, especially as we move toward a more virtual world. I always try to keep an eye out to see if people are checking emails while I'm talking or if I see puzzled faces looking back at me. Or is it all head nods and smiles? The more I can try to stay present when speaking and cognizant of how those around me are taking in the information, the better I find the content gets delivered. It is truly amazing how other people's facial cues can help signal when it's time to pick up the pace or to wrap it up. Also, nods of comprehension or encouragement can signal me to keep going.

And keep going, I did. That second day of work was not the last time I'd find myself in a new or intimidating business meeting. With each meeting comes new learnings and—let's face it—new stories!

Chapter 4

BUILDING A SUPPORT NETWORK

A good friend, mentor, and former manager often reminds me of the old African proverb, "If you want to go fast, go alone; but if you want to go far, go together." Of course, this adage can manifest itself in many ways, most often associated with teamwork. However, I use it here to demonstrate the importance of building a support network because that is one thing—no matter what your career path is—that, without it, you are most certain to fail. Like friends, colleagues come into your life for a reason, a season, or a lifetime. I have been blessed to have been surrounded by incredible colleagues over the years, many of whom fall into all three of those categories. I have also come to learn how important it is to have different levels and types of support.

I remember many nights—in all my jobs—leaving the office late with bleary eyes, my head spinning, and in need of a good rant over something outrageous that happened that day or had been building up that I let fester inside of me.

In that first job, the first phone call I would typically make—while jaywalking across Third Avenue—was to my mom, who always allowed me to vent. Here's how it would generally go: When I tell her I am quitting my job, she first tells me to stop walking into oncoming traffic (she hears the horns and you can sense the panic in her voice) and then tells me to get home safe, take a shower, eat dinner, relax, watch some TV or read a book, and get a good night's sleep. Her advice is solid in that respect, and she tries, but as a reading specialist at a school, she is in a very different profession and doesn't *really* get all that my job entails.

The next call or text would be to a peer, those I look for when it comes to guidance. My peers always bring me back to reality. They've typically been there themselves. They have the necessary perspective. One peer in particular was always my go-to in these types of situations. I'd share my qualm of the moment.

"Really?" She'd say, giving me that side-eye look.

"Meh. I know. I am overreacting, right?"

"Yeah. You have to think about it from this perspective . . ." And then she'd go on with some sage advice.

I really wasn't going to quit my job. I knew that. My mom did too when I called her to rant. But it's the peer who got through to me. After a virtual slap in the face that brought me back to reality, I did everything else my mother suggested I do. And tomorrow was a new day.

Inevitably, a few days later I would be fine and then I'd play the same role for my peer over coffee (or tea for me, as I don't drink coffee) in a bougie coffee house, lunch in a New York-style deli, or dinner in a sticky diner booth in Midtown East. Occasionally we would treat ourselves to a finer meal in one of New York City's trendy, of-the-moment hotspots or swanky cocktail bars. We'd have said conversation over an over-priced fusion meal or a fancy libation made with ingredients I'd never heard of, or never would have thought to put together.

I am always grateful to have support from outside the working world—friends and family—and I am not downplaying their roles and importance. However, the value of a peer is sometimes superior when it comes to career planning and advice. What I have found is that you need someone at or around your level who is experiencing similar things to you, and is in your field or a similar field, so they understand your world and the context. It's sometimes even more helpful if they understand the players.

This person isn't a buddy who you only complain to—although let's be honest—a lot of that is going to happen. This person is a colleague who can help you by providing perspective, bringing you back to reality when you've gone too far, helping make your work stronger, or helping take you in another direction when you go off course.

One major caveat: I learned over time that it is best if this person is not on your direct team, as that can sometimes lead to unintentionally creating a negative environment where you bring each other and the team down instead of up.

At my first job, I was incredibly fortunate to have three ladies who started around the same time as me. All 2010 grads, we were the same age and coming up in the ranks together. I can still vividly picture the late nights in the office—we were heads down at work, but it made it better to know you had a friend just a few cubicles away. Together, we ordered takeout food, went out for late night drinks, and took our friendships outside the workplace on off hours to enjoy the days of being young and single in New York City.

I remember having the deepest of conversations with this crew—ranging from what we wanted out of our future careers to what we wanted in life.

It never crossed my mind that these ladies would forever become part of my professional network, which was rapidly forming before my eyes. Aside from having their support to get through the day-to-day in those early years, some of them became the gateway to forming my future network. We would introduce each other to people and open doors for each other. We still do to this day.

As they say, "The only thing in life that is constant is change." One of the truest adages out there. And because you never know when change will strike you or someone else around you, having a strong network can also come in handy in these times of need.

As important as your peers are, the support network does extend beyond. From the early days, I've always had a mentor. My first mentor was assigned, and thankfully, the pairing worked out well. This mentor provided much-needed perspective from someone who was further along in their career, helping me to understand the bigger picture of how things worked in those early days. We would talk about everything from life at an agency to how to handle certain client situations. It helped that we naturally got along, so the conversation was never stale or awkward.

My mentor and I would make it a point to take our conversations outside the office. In these early years, I appreciated someone who made the time to teach me more, beyond just the craft. She taught me how to take a break—eating lunch outside the office, going for a walk, or grabbing a coffee (*tea!*) from a local shop versus the office machine.

We always conveniently timed our lunch sessions to the "NYC Restaurant Week" calendar in February and August. Over Italian food at Lavo or surf-and-turf at Smith and Wollensky, she listened to my gripes with open ears and shared her perspective. She built me up and encouraged me to keep after the things I wanted, but she was also real with me when I was looking at certain situations with too narrow of a view.

Nowadays, I am incredibly lucky to have a few wonderful mentors. Although my experience with the agency match was a positive one, ironically I never participated in a company mentor match program again. I have nothing against them. In fact, I applaud them and highly recommend them, as they provide access to mentees who otherwise may go without a mentor and vice versa. It is an opportunity for professionals to impart their wisdom to others that otherwise may have gone unheard. It is also an amazing way to navigate a new company as a newcomer or gain insight into another department if your mentor comes from another area of a business. I just felt like I needed someone who I had already built a rapport with, knew my areas of strength and opportunity, and could therefore provide a specific type of perspective—and maybe most important, who could be brutally honest with me.

There's also another important category that consists of those who are a few years above you and work with you, but don't manage you directly. They may not be an official mentor, but they can become a valuable source to learn from.

On June 2, 2010, I had no idea how I was going to be a contributing member of the account dealing with home loans. By June 4, 2010, I knew I was going to be okay. Why? Because I had two incredible colleagues a few years older than me who took it upon themselves to show me the ropes. Both, in their own ways, would find the time to teach me what I needed to know. They explained in layman's terms and laughed along with me, not at me. After all, they assured me that they too had no clue about the mysterious world of mortgages until they found themselves in a similar situation as me.

I am forever indebted to all the colleagues I've met along the way who took the time to teach and explain, and made me feel part of the team instead of making me feel small, or less than, for not already knowing what they knew.

The support network should also include your manager. I have come to find that the best managers are the ones you can learn from—the good and the bad habits. I've found this to be so important, particularly as I, myself, progressed toward becoming a manager. It's crucial to note what you like about managers and what are your criticisms. For too long, it became an unhealthy habit to stew in the criticisms until I realized they could be used for something productive. Write these things down. Remember what you don't like about it and why. And then, when you ultimately end up replicating that behavior down the road on your own direct-reports, give yourself a slap on the wrist. Just as we recognize sometimes how we're turning into our parents, this too will happen in the professional world. And it will be a tough pill to swallow when you realize it.

Over the years, I learned that a good manager takes the time to understand you—"What are your goals? Future aspirations?"—and helps you get there. At one specific moment in time, I found myself feeling stuck. Instead of using the annual personal development plan exercise as a "check the box," my manager at the time took it upon herself to help me create clarity and a real plan. She asked me to start by identifying my values and strengths, what activities at work gave me energy, and conversely, what drained my energy (my personal favorite of all the lists), and what did I want out of my next role? This process forced me to think. To really think.

I ended up with a list of raw, authentic thoughts and desires, which included things that you would expect and things that were unique and personal to me. Items like:

Energy giver:

- Fast-paced projects that come with complexity and a level of difficulty that provide a thrill
- Opportunity to shape and create something truly from the ground up
- Fitting all the pieces of a complicated jigsaw puzzle together to make sense of something
- Being around others with contagious energy, drive, and ambition

Energy drainer:

- Mundane tasks that come with too much bureaucracy
- Situations that cause more or unnecessary work due to inefficiency or lack of vision
- Meetings that are a waste of time
- Too many details or processes that restrict freedom and lead to a feeling of being stuck in someone else's box

Desires for the next role:

- A role I can truly grow into; where the ceiling is not already within reach when I start so I can spend a few years (3+) really learning and growing
- A role where I can shape a program or an agenda and leave a lasting impact (for the right reasons) to help a business excel

- A role where I can dip my toes into unfamiliar territory to learn something new while having just enough sense of familiarity to fall back on

- A role that continuously comes with big, complex problems to solve

I had no idea at the time how creating a list like this in the present would help me so much in the future, but this document was to become my navigation map for the years to come. It is all thanks to having a great manager who stepped out of the day-to-day to take the time to have this conversation with me.

I also learned that a good manager can celebrate the wins and, just as effectively, tactfully point out the learnings. Instead of competing, even if key colleagues are the same, a good manager creates space for you to shine and recognizes that there is room for all to succeed. When you realize you can always learn something from everyone you encounter, and you open your mind to embrace this, you can have a positive experience—even with the worst of managers or senior colleagues. These are all traits I take with me as I continue on my own journey as a manager.

At different times in my career, I have found myself in some situations where I was reporting to a manager who had once been a peer, or the nature of the relationship was previously very different.

In my experience, working for a good friend *is* possible. But this is something I picked up along the way. Most often, the hard way.

I learned that it doesn't work if you don't set guardrails from the onset. So how would this actually work? In order to establish a good working relationship, I learned that you not only *need* to have these tough conversations, you need to do it *before* the change in work relationship formally begins. How does each person like to get feedback? How often? Do you keep work-related matters to office hours and personal-related matters to outside office hours? Is the person who is the manager aware of your own personal career goals? What motivates you? What motivates them? Is there mutual trust and respect inside and outside of the workplace? Is there space for both of you to learn and grow? And to shine?

I also learned that it absolutely does not work or help anyone in the situation to hold things back—the good, the bad, and the ugly! Constant open communication is key, even if it is often uncomfortable.

In one situation, I went in knowing a guardrail conversation needed to take place, but I shied away from it. I thought I could work around it, and by showing this friend-turned-line manager I had full trust in them, I thought it could be avoided altogether. The conversation never happened at the onset of the new working relationship, and because of that, it led to some rocky situations for both of us. When things were good, they were really good. After all, we worked well together and complemented each other. This we already knew, as we had the opportunity to work as peers previously. However, when things were bad, it was like oil and vinegar, and you could feel the tension building.

At a certain point in time, I mustered up the courage to tell it like it is. It was incredibly difficult. I didn't want to hurt my "friend-ager," my line manager, whom I still considered a good friend, yet I knew if I wasn't brutally honest about how things were going from my perspective, the professional and personal relationship would likely be tarnished forever. Additionally, if I continued to keep it in, the negative feelings spiraling inside of me could contribute to my own demise or unnecessary self-departure from the company.

In this situation, the conversation took place about eighteen months past due. It was January—the start of a new year. What better time to reset? I didn't want to place blame on anyone. I just wanted to finally break the silence, acknowledge the uncomfortable situation, and share how I was feeling.

I wrote out what I wanted to say first to organize my thoughts. I remember feeling incredibly nervous. In the moment, I would've given anything to unwind the clock and never have hit send on the calendar invite to have the conversation. "How to begin" raced through my mind, even though I had practiced my opening lines over and over in my head in the days and sleepless nights leading up to the call. My heart fluttered as I began; my palms were sweaty. I opened my mouth, my voice a bit shaky, and leaned in.

I shared my honest thoughts. I remember mentioning exactly how I felt: "When we worked well, we were on fire, but when there was tension, it felt like skating on thin ice."

I recall putting the idea out there that it might be best if I were to go, even though I didn't know what would be next. At the same time, I also wanted to get the message across that I believed this could work, because I did truly believe that. I also believed that something—on both ends—had to change to achieve that.

As difficult as it was for me to have this conversation—perhaps the most difficult in my career to date—I can only imagine how difficult it was for my manager on the receiving end. However, I believe it had an incredibly positive outcome for both of us. It saved our working relationship and made our friendship even stronger.

Through our discussion, we realized we needed to set up separate times to check in and reflect on our working relationship throughout the course of the year. This would be different than the day-to-day catch-ups about active projects. This was time meant to *really* check in: How was the relationship going? Anything either of us wanted to raise? Was there any recent feedback to give in either direction—positive or negative?

Sometimes tough conversations are just that—tough. I find, though, that they are usually incredibly worth it in the end. This particular conversation ultimately changed the face of the relationship I had with my then-manager in the best way possible. I cannot imagine what the following months would have looked like had we not had this conversation. To this day, I am incredibly lucky to still call this former manager a now mentor and good friend.

Would I recommend getting yourself into this situation in the first place? It depends. Sometimes it happens organically, and sometimes you have a choice. Having been there, I would try my best to avoid it again. I do think it is an invitation for unnecessary tension and frustration in your life that, really, no one needs. But should it happen, at least I know

I have learned what works and what doesn't work and will be better prepared to handle it.

Everyone is going to have bad days. It happens to all of us, and unfortunately, it happens throughout our careers. If you're sitting there saying, "This doesn't happen to me," you're either lying to yourself or you're not human. Had it not been for the support system I surrounded myself with over the years, I am not sure I would've made it through the toughest of days, endlessly long nights, crazy cycles of travel, issues and crises management, and more that arose over the years.

I still count my lucky stars for those peers, mentors, and managers who have gone from colleagues to lifelong mentors and friends. I recognize that it doesn't always happen that way, and I realize how lucky I am to have found such relationships several times over.

Chapter 5

IDENTIFYING EARLY SUPERPOWERS

W hen you start out in the world of PR and communications, your first job will largely be spent "monitoring."

Monitoring. The dreaded word to any entry-level communications pro. Monitoring essentially means scouring the news to

1. keep track of your client(s) in the news;

2. understand which journalists cover your beat, what they are interested in writing about, and in which newspaper, magazine, or online source they publish in; and

3. identify creative trends and crack potential angles that you can use to proactively pitch your client/brand to the media and/or leverage to create campaigns.

Monitoring is one of the most tedious, time-consuming tasks that a junior employee at a PR agency has to do. Even in today's world of Google Alerts, Factiva, Cision, and more, monitoring is nonnegotiable.

I just called this task "tedious," so it would make sense why one would hate indulging in the task, right? It would never top the most useful skills list, right? WRONG.

I quickly learned that mastering the mundane, in my case, "monitoring," is the single best way to make your talents known early on. After all, you are harnessing the insights that will drive the team's strategy. In my case, I was collecting fodder that was going to strengthen media pitches and land media coverage. I realized I was the driving force behind the team, and I had the power to help the team win big.

In my first few months on the job following college, I was like any regular entry-level, young PR professional. I couldn't believe I needed a college education to scour the news to learn about things like travel industry trends, what our competitors were up to, and finding and capturing mentions of our clients (usually placed by us!) to be shared with said client or held onto for our own records.

In one of my very first days in the real world, a colleague was teaching me the art of making a mockup. This was essentially creating a clean screenshot of the online news articles, blog posts, video content, etc. to save as a JPG or PDF file for later use in coverage reports. She was offloading the task, and although it must've been a glorious feeling for her, she had a heart, and I distinctly remember her looking at me and saying, "I know, not the most stimulating task. Can't believe you need a fancy college degree for this, huh?!"

Soon after, the pieces of the puzzle started to fall into place for me. I realized how to turn this mundane task into an incredibly useful skill—some might even call it a superpower. As I learned more about my client's business, I got more creative in how I used my monitoring. I quickly realized the value it brought to the team. Instead of falling into the minutia of the mundane, I started to find ways to elevate my thinking and challenge myself to put his newfound knowledge to good use. I began to appreciate the strategic role I could play through a very tactical assignment given to the youngest person in the room.

In doing so, the little nuggets I would share at team meetings would get played back in other, more strategic forms. Sometimes these set the foundation for our annual plans, project proposals, and new business pitches.

Think about it. Since the beginning of time, we've been told that knowledge is power. Why wouldn't you want to be the one positively fueling the knowledge engine on your team?

Being the youngest—or most junior person—in the room is actually a very powerful position. Are you the one taking the notes? Great! This means you are also the one who can do the first reflection and proactively come up with an idea for how to take a project forward. Did you write something down you didn't fully understand or need clarity on? Fantastic! Use that as a moment to do some research—either on your own or ask questions—to further educate yourself and your understanding of the business. What did you hear in the room? Do you agree, or do you see things from a different perspective? Are older generations trying to crack the code on reaching those from *your* generation but going down the wrong path? Speak up! How can your own personal anecdotes fuel the conversation further? Those who can see past the minutia of the task at hand—in my case, scouring the news to monitor for client mentions—and can understand the influence they hold—in my case, sharing valuable insights to inform strategy—are likely the ones who are going to succeed.

This is advice I gave over and over again to interns and junior employees alike, as I, myself, began rising through the ranks during my agency days and had the luxury of offloading the task of monitoring. Like any other piece of advice, some chose to take it, and some just continued to complain. Some of those who I knew understood what I was saying are VPs and SVPs now, running teams of their own at agencies or thriving at in-house jobs. Some hold higher rank in terms of position than I do today. Seeing them succeed and knowing I may have played even the smallest role in their early days is, quite frankly, one of the most gratifying feelings in the world.

❧

If there is power in learning to appreciate the mundane and turn it into an opportunity for your own growth, there's also power in learning how to grow from being uncomfortable. Enter superpower number 2: embracing the uncomfortable state of being uncomfortable.

Over the years, I experienced many uncomfortable moments that I now identify as being real challenges. When I think of the times I was truly challenged, my mind takes me way back before my professional days. I am instantly transported to the eleventh grade. Chemistry class. The classroom is in one of the newer wings of the buildings with central air conditioning, and it's cold.

I am good at many things. Science is not one of them. I am struggling. I also do not like being cold, and I am always cold. The subject matter *and* the air temperature send a chill up my spine. I am physically and mentally uncomfortable.

My teacher repeats over and over, "Just do the work." At this time, I do not know what he means. I disregard his words and consider them annoying. Wasn't I doing that? I always do my work. I do my homework; I study. With every other subject, that works, and I succeed.

However, every other subject comes with more ease. If I study for a French test for twenty minutes, I probably will score 92–94 percent on my exam. If I study for forty-five minutes, I'm looking at a 98–100 percent with a chance to score over 100 percent if I get the bonus question right. That's good enough for me. After all, I am a busy teen. I have soccer practice and/or games five days a week, choir practice on Monday evening, acting class on Wednesday evening, and rehearsals for the two shows I am in (at the same time) four-to-five times a week. Oh, and I also have friends.

I finally found something that stopped me in my tracks—chemistry—and I didn't like it. If I studied more, it didn't seem to pay off. If I went for extra help, the concepts still blurred in my mind. I just wasn't wired to understand chemistry, while everyone around me seemed to float by.

It was an unfamiliar feeling. I felt like a failure. I felt stupid. I didn't know how to handle it, and I couldn't figure out how to get it to turn in my favor. I had lost control, which didn't sit well with someone who was always very in control.

I happily moved on after that year and never looked back. It wouldn't be until years later that I could finally make some sense of it all and understand what I had experienced.

I started a new professional role in early 2017, and I was being challenged for the first time in a while. It was in this moment that I reached a standstill that made me go back all those years to the eleventh-grade chemistry lab problem. I finally realized that it was one of the first moments in my life where I was uncomfortable because I was *actually* being challenged.

Challenges come in all shapes and forms. In the case of my days in chemistry class, I was forced to think differently. What do you do when what you have always done isn't working? As a junior in high school, I didn't devote the time needed to master it, and I truly didn't have the patience to figure it out. I stayed the course and tried to study the same way I always did. I was blind to the idea of flexing my style of learning, and therefore I didn't ask the right questions or seek out the right resources. In many ways, I was also overthinking, which caused a whole slew of other issues and insecurities:

Why do I not understand this when I understand everything else? As any sixteen-year-old believes they understand or know everything.

Maybe I am stupid.

Am I stupid?

Will I get into college now?

Will I succeed in life?

Why is this happening to me? My friends in my other more advanced classes have no problems here.

I must be stupid.

I was experiencing the dark spiral of anxiety, believing my own insecurities, and falling into the evil trap of comparison against my peers. If only I could have taken a breath and embraced the challenge in front of me. If only I could have taken a step back, reassessed, and then tried—really tried—to figure it out.

I was also learning to embrace failure. No, I didn't fail the course numerically, but I failed by my own standards. The final grade was by no means a shiny star on my report card. In fact, I saw it as a dark spot on my otherwise pretty solid record. I had to accept it at the end of the term, as the grade had such finality to it—there was no way to improve it after the term had ended. It would forever be etched in my record. That was another tough pill to swallow at a young age.

In those days, my coping mechanism was to forget that the incident—or the year-long torment—had happened and move on without ever looking back. Little did I know how significant this experience would be for me later in life, or how the torment of the words "do the work" from my teacher would haunt my dreams in the years to come.

So, what does it mean to do the work? To be honest, I still do not know *exactly* what my teacher meant, but I do know how I interpret that advice now. To me, it means there are no shortcuts in life. I find this to be especially true now in the working world. It means sometimes you need more patience, you need to change your approach, or you need to ask different questions. It also means that sometimes you will encounter a challenge you cannot overcome. Or not at 100 percent anyway. And maybe that's okay.

I can't help but smile at the discomfort I felt at the time sitting at my desk in that classroom and how I now run toward challenges in the workplace with open arms. This doesn't necessarily mean taking on more and biting off more than you can chew. That's just a recipe for disaster. Trust me—been there, done that. It means finding the challenges that will complement your strengths, teach you something new, and stretch you in ways you did not imagine possible.

What did I learn from this? There are things in life that will come easier than others. I need to do those things and do them well. And because I'm a speed demon, I need to do them quickly to feel the rush that comes with it. I need those things to keep going and boost my confidence. But I won't be fooled; these are not the things that are stretching me or preparing me for that next promotion.

There will also be things in life that will not come with such ease. I may want to run the other way from them, bury them on my to-do list and pretend they don't exist, or try to offload them onto someone else. I've learned to embrace them because those are the things that will help me learn and grow. I've learned to take the time these tasks demand. Do the work. It is okay to ask for help, support, or guidance. I do not have to do it on my own.

It is also okay not to know what to do. It is okay to ask the questions you may be holding onto because you don't want to be perceived as dumb. It's okay to take a stab at a first draft, put it in front of your boss with the caveat it's half-baked and ask for support to work through it together. It doesn't have to be perfect the first time around. In fact, even if you know what you are doing, it is rarely perfect the first time around, and it is likely that it is never going to be perfect. I also learned that not everything has to be done at 110 percent.

Most importantly, I learned that when I stop learning and growing, when I am too comfortable, that is when I know I need to find my next challenge.

And in that discomfort, there is power.

❄

While there is power in the mundane and uncomfortable, perhaps the greatest superpower I *started* to learn in my early years is how to say "No!"

If the first three years of my career were about kickstarting it and learning the ropes, I spent the next seven learning from failure. And failure, as I learned early on in the chemistry lab, will always be part of life and every job. If you learn from it, you grow. If you don't, maybe you need to build more reflection time into your day-to-day regimen or ask for more feedback.

In the millennial world in which I grew up, I, like so many others, blame the lack of ability to innately recognize failure on the participation trophy. The participation trophy was given out to every kid for showing up instead of those who actually earned it. Does putting a miniscule piece of plastic or metal that you didn't deserve on top of your bookshelf make you feel accomplished? To a seven-year-old, perhaps. Most certainly, the negative long-term impact was something no one considered when they started doling out these prizes for substandard performance on the field, court, or stage.

Anyway, I've often wondered what it is about the word failure that has such a negative connotation. It's a harsh term. No one likes to fail. No one likes to lose. As many wise people in my life along the way have said, "Words matter."

So, what if we stopped calling them "failures" and instead started calling them "learnings"? What would that do? Would people be more reflective in the workplace? Would they be more willing to share what they have learned with colleagues and peers? My hypothesis would be yes, but clearly, as you have probably learned, I am no scientist.

One of my biggest educations to date was developing the ability to say no. The *in*ability to say no is crippling and damaging. Not only is this true for yourself, but it can also impact those around you.

If the truth be told, I am still learning how to say no. However, once I started doing it, I realized how much empowerment it brought. The first few times I successfully said no, I felt physically lighter. The stress and tension in my body went away, and I wasn't so anxious all the time. I felt like I had gained control of my calendar and was able to bring balance back into my life.

This epiphany didn't happen overnight. Quite the contrary. This epiphany came from ten long years of learning and dozens of managers, mentors, and peers telling me I needed to do it, and finally, several run-ins with burnout.

I could share thousands of stories of times when I should've said no. *Should've, could've, would've* . . . but didn't say no.

One specific example comes to mind. I was still pretty young and about four years into my career. I was working on an exciting project for a client who was a sponsor of the US Soccer Federation and gearing up to launch a campaign that spring for the 2014 Men's FIFA World Cup. As part of the campaign, the client had access to two US men's national team players for media interviews. In the world of PR, this is pure gold. The challenge is usually that the time blocks you have with these talents are extremely narrow and limited, so you must do whatever you need to do quickly and efficiently within the allotted time.

We had access to one player in NYC on—let's call it day one—tied to the big fanfare happening before the US team left for Brazil. We would also have access to another player on day two because we had landed a rare opportunity to do a live TV interview with *E!* for its nightly TV program . . . in LA. This meant a very full first day of running around Times Square with Talent No. 1 and getting in three-to-four interviews with top-tier media like the *New York Times*. Then I had to gun it to the airport to board a 5:30 p.m. flight to LAX for a twenty-minute TV interview with Talent No. 2 in the morning (day two) in LA. Afterward, I would need to rush back to the airport for a noon flight back to NYC, as we would be jumping into the next project for a different client already on day three of that week.

Back in those days, I took pride in my "no rest for the weary" attitude. I truly lived the "you'll sleep when dead" mentality. Now I look back and realize just how dumb I was. I also realize how much harm we bring to ourselves because we think we need to when no one is asking us to. As soon as I knew what this schedule would entail, I should have rethought the plan because it was too much for one person.

In reality, I had an exhausting yet successful day one, and I was thinking, *Go me!* I had to make a mad dash to the airport in rush hour traffic, with my heart fluttering because I was convinced that I was going to miss this flight. Forehead drenched, I somehow made it into my seat before takeoff, where the flight attendant was already by my side, asking me personally to power down my electronics.

These were also the days when I would shower with my BlackBerry propped up right outside the shower so I could watch for the little red light indicating I had a new email. The job was demanding, and my team was intense, but once again, I was the one who set my own limits, or lack thereof. I just didn't know that back then. I didn't think I had the power to do so. I didn't think my life was my own.

Not being able to check my email before taking off on the five-plus-hour flight gave me a complete heart attack because I knew the West Coast-based producer would likely be emailing about last-minute details for the next day's interview. Had I set these expectations with my colleagues and asked them to be "on call" while I was in flight, a big problem could have been avoided.

After the panic subsided, I was almost relieved. They didn't have the internet widely available on domestic flights back then. This meant I would have five full hours to get some work done that didn't require the internet and then maybe, just maybe, some time to close my eyes and get some rest. And God knew I needed it. So, off the grid I went . . .

Following an on-time flight, I found myself in LA. I had a plan to grab dinner with two of my good friends as soon as I landed, and then head straight to the hotel for some sleep the night before a full day two. Except that when I landed, there were streams of emails, voicemails, and texts with more to-dos for tomorrow's event. In that instant, not yet off the plane—in fact, not even technically allowed to turn the phones on yet—the plane transformed into a ship. I instantly felt like we had wrecked and I was washed up on a deserted island. I felt the weight of the world on my shoulders. I felt completely alone.

Also, remember that I *ran* to the plane hours earlier. I was completely disheveled and had been sitting in my own sweat for several hours.

How did I get here? It was because I didn't set boundaries. I never said no. I never asked for help. I said yes with a smile. I thought I could do it all, and do it all well.

I called my two LA dinner friends—the ones who had become family years earlier and very important members of my support network. And because it was them, I was wailing by this point because I was so tired and overwhelmed, and I smelled! I was still sitting on the plane and told them I couldn't meet. Older and wiser, they said, "Stop. You're coming over. We'll order in. You cannot go sit in a hotel alone like this. You need to eat, and you need to take a break. We'll talk you through it."

They saved me that night. I was so lucky to have them. I am still so lucky to have them. They told me that I needed to change my ways. They were not the first and, unfortunately, not the last. But something they said got through. I was *starting* to get it.

Anyone wondering how the *E!* shoot on day two went? It was really great. Soccer Talent No. 2 was a terrific spokesperson and a pleasure to be around. We got to kick around the ball a bit together as we prepped, and the interviewer had a lot of fun on the makeshift pitch on the rooftop of the hotel. All went off without a hitch. We did what we needed to do, and there I was, back at LAX less than eighteen hours after I had arrived.

After that whole West Coast ordeal, I still had the toughest part awaiting me: confronting the learning curve I had just lived through, and some unhappy colleagues in New York. I arrived back in the office the next day—still exhausted and already onto the next project.

While inside a creative agency, there were boundless nooks and crannies to set up shop that took you to a different space to work than your desk. I remember dropping my bag at my desk, grabbing my laptop, and gravitating to a different section in the office as soon as I got in. I didn't want to see anyone. My manager came and sat with me later in the day. I told her I had taken on too much and that I never should've agreed to staff both days of events. In doing so, I also realized I had taken opportunities away from junior members of the team. Maybe someone else wanted to do the NYC part or the LA part? Or join me in NYC to learn, if they hadn't already experienced such a media relations-heavy program with top-tier media like this before.

For the rest of the afternoon, and a while after, I felt the tail between my legs. It was a hard lesson to learn. But I learned. Kind of. Like I said earlier, working on saying no is something I am still—and probably always will be—working on. In some instances, it is easier to flex this muscle, and in other instances, it is still extremely difficult. And that is okay. I know that many others struggle with it as well. All I can say is that instead of beating myself up, I celebrate my ability to at least recognize it now and try my best to stop it in its tracks before it flares up again.

Chapter 6

EVERYTHING I LEARNED IN LIFE, I LEARNED FROM BROADWAY

In the field of communications and corporate affairs, it is important that we consistently bring what is happening in the outside world into the boardroom—from pop culture to politics. This is why finding power in the mundane early on was a skill that would set me up for future success, even though I didn't know it at the time.

This is particularly true nowadays, as the world around us changes so fast. Mechanisms for reaching consumers and customers come and go with the wind, and we need to know how to strategically partner with our colleagues to guide decisions on what topics to address and where to place our message.

However, when it comes to the world of pop culture, this has always been a struggle for me. It's not that I am unaware of the world around me, but I am the type who would rather go for a run listening to a classic Broadway musical soundtrack than the latest on the top songs of the week list. I couldn't care less about which celebrities are now dating, what they are wearing, and who showed up at which party. And I can't be bothered to keep up with the ever-growing roster of A-list celebrities. I'd rather read a historical fiction novel than a magazine.

This is something that several colleagues have found completely fascinating about me over the years. I vividly remember a former boss and now good friend marveling at the fact I am "pop culture illiterate, yet so successful in my job."

Although my appetite for pop culture is underwhelmingly low, I can clearly appreciate how bringing the outside in can help in a multitude of ways, so I work hard to find ways to educate myself to stay relevant.

Yes, I know what *The Bachelor* is. *No*, you still won't catch me watching it on Monday night.

But I also refuse to give up on what makes me unique, and how I prefer to spend my free time. Therefore, I find ways to bring what I do know to the table. In this case, I am talking specifically about Broadway! Teachers, mentors, and bosses—they have all taught me a lot—but really, I credit most of what I've learned in this world to Broadway. And to me, Broadway counts as pop culture as well.

I was started on the Broadway train at an early age. My family had a mutual love and admiration for Broadway, and having showtunes playing in the background in our house was not uncommon. By the time I was four, I knew every word to *Les Misérables*. So naturally, when I was five or six, I begged my parents to take me to see it.

My Nana reacted as any sensible adult by asking Mom, "You're taking five and eight-year-olds to see a show about a revolution? Are you nuts?" But we went—prostitutes, barricades, suicide, romance, and all.

Of course, to me and my sister, knowing every word to the songs didn't correlate to understanding most of what was happening on stage at our young ages. I was fixated by Young Cosette, Young Eponine, and Gavroche—there were kids like me on stage! And *wow*—what a set. The music, those voices. I did not, however, enjoy the gunshots during the scenes at the barricade. To this day, when I see a *Les Mis* production, I still jump upon hearing the sound reverberate throughout the theater.

Over the years, my love for *Les Misérables* turned into a love for all theater, and the songs and soundtracks that stuck in my head helped broaden my vocabulary, took me to faraway places, and helped me build a genuine appreciation for the world. I admired the creativity of everyone who had a hand in every production. The genius it takes to put on a show is similar to the creativity it takes to build a new brand or put a brand in the spotlight. And let's not forget the importance of storytelling in the workplace. Whether a live musical or play, we can all learn a thing or two, in the audience of a well-done production, on how to tell—or sell—a story. No matter what industry you are in, and no matter what your profession, the art of being able to tell a story is a skill that can take you far.

Over the years, knowing the words to hundreds of Broadway scores has helped me in life. I spotted words on my college SAT that I knew the context of because of showtunes. Maybe one of my favorite "because of Broadway" stories is about being able to safely navigate my friend and I from London to Paris via an impromptu trip to Calais, France.

When I was studying abroad in London (more on that later), my friend and I were going to visit another friend who was studying in Paris. As we headed to St. Pancras to catch the Eurostar, we were informed that there was a fire in the Chunnel and all trains were canceled. Thankfully no one was injured, but that was definitely unfortunate for all trying to travel over the next twenty-four hours.

At the station, the attendants directed us to trains that would take us to Dover—on the southeast coast of the United Kingdom—and then we were to take ferry boats to Calais. I could see the panic in my friend's eyes. *Calais? What and where is Calais?!*

My mind was immediately whizzing through the lyrics for the lead-in to "One Day More" from *Les Mis*. At this midway point of the show, former convict-turned-mayor, Jean Valjean, is misled by his daughter, Cosette, that she had screamed to turn away an unwanted visitor. She was covering for the fact that her newfound love, Marius, had snuck into the garden for a visit, which was welcomed by Cosette, but would've been unwelcomed by Jean Valjean. In telling this white lie, her father's alarm bells go off, as he still, technically, is a convict on the run. His instinct is that they must flee. They must run from the shadows of the past or they'll never find rest. He suggests heading to the coast—to Calais—where they can take a ship across the English Channel to England.

Oh yes, Calais. By process of deductive reasoning, I knew Calais must be on the northwest coast of France, and an easy gateway from France to the UK across the English Channel. Here we were on the UK side. We were enacting Jean Valjean's plan in reverse!

Okay, I could work with this. I assured my friend I knew where we were going and how to navigate us to Paris via train from Calais.

The journey included ending up on the wrong, more luxurious ferry to France after never having purchased a ticket, and several train transfers where, once again, we did not have the proper tickets. Our luck almost ran out on the last leg as we approached Paris and the conductor asked for our "billets." Instead of attempting to explain the situation in my rusty French, I did what any other panicky twenty-year-old would do: claim to not speak French and just repeat the word Paris and point to our now defunct Eurostar tickets. He was noticeably irritated with us but eventually gave up and moved on. And as promised to my friend, I proudly delivered us to the platform at Gare du Nord, where, several hours later and through broken communication (our rented Nokia cell phones hadn't gotten us too far), miraculously, our friend was still there awaiting our arrival.

And then there was the time I went for my first professional audition. *The Lion King* was having "open calls" for kids to audition for Young Simba and Young Nala. An open call means you didn't need a theatrical agent to secure the audition for you—although I was hell-bent on having an agent at the time.

I convinced my parents to take me to said audition. It was held in a school in Jamaica, Queens, and the line to get in wrapped several times around a long city block. We were there, and I was not leaving until I was seen, even though I was the wrong age (too old at eleven years old), too tall (as age could've been ignored if I was shorter), and the wrong ethnicity.

I remember exactly what I wore—floral patterned pants, black Steve

Madden platform shoes, a turquoise-colored Juicy Couture cardigan set that brought out my eyes, and a "bra strap" headband to hold my frizzy red hair back—*yes*, that was the trend at the time. I was a New York nineties pre-teen through and through.

After what seemed like an eternity, I was placed in a group that was sent in for the first part of the audition. The director placed us in a circle—the pianist started to play the notes for "I Just Can't Wait to Be King." You had to pay attention, as the director would point to you, and you had to pick up where the last kid left off. I sang my little heart out. The adrenaline was racing, my heart pumping. I felt so alive. I hit every note. It felt like I had this in the bag.

What happened next was a character-building moment. The director split us into two groups. He said those who received stickers were to move on to the next round, the dance audition, and those who did not receive stickers could find their parents and go home. That would be all.

I stood up proud and tall as the director approached me with the roll of stickers. Standing tall was probably not the wisest thing to do in this situation, given I was already heads taller than the other kids around me. Anyway, I had a beaming smile plastered on my face as the sticker was placed on my chest. But just as quickly as the adhesive side was settling into my cotton cardigan, it was being peeled off. My heart sank, and the smile dissipated.

"Sorry, wrong group," someone in the back called out.

Ouch! The sting of rejection in its purest form.

I like to think that was the director's way of saying, "Sorry kid, you were good, but this is not your moment. Keep at it!" Or something along those lines . . . Deep down I knew this wasn't the role for me, but I went and I tried. It was a learning and growth moment, if ever there was one, and I enjoyed every minute of being in that room. It was another way in which Broadway shaped me.

What does this have to do with anything about thriving in the workplace? Aside from the enjoyment I get in regaling people with these stories and showcasing how being a Broadway buff can come in handy just as much as being up to speed on the latest in pop culture, it goes to show how all our experiences in life—even the most seemingly trivial events from a long time ago—can play a role in shaping us. We just need to be open to taking it all in, and then, of course, digging it out of our brains and applying the learning when the time is right.

It's also helped foster connection over the years and drive conversation amongst clients and colleagues alike inside and outside the boardroom. And my random facts, song lyrics, eclectic vocabulary, and storylines have led to creative ideas in brainstorms, discussions, and plans.

It was beyond thrilling when *Hamilton* broke the lines between Broadway and pop culture, and as entertainment lines continue to blur, I hope to see more of that in the years to come.

I also suppose, in a way, that the real learning here for myself was about being true to yourself. We all have little quirks that make us who we are. You never know when Broadway knowledge will be needed, so why would I trade it to become an expert on something I'm not totally interested in? But if you work in any industry in today's world that is so driven by cultural relevance, you probably *should* know a little something about pop culture too. And boy am I thankful *Hamilton* put Broadway back in the pop culture vernacular!

Chapter 7

THE YOUNGEST ONE IN THE ROOM: ANOTHER ENCOUNTER

Jumping back to my first job, I'd like to think I was starting to get the hang of this PR agency thing. Around this point in time, I was given a compliment that came in the ultimate form of flattery—not a promotion, not a raise. No. I was invited to join the annual plan presentation that was being given to the most senior client on one of my accounts. I had worked hard the last fifteen months and built a solid relationship with my clients, but had limited exposure to this particular client.

Wow! I was elated.

I should also assure you that, by this point in time, I was no longer commuting and/or squatting at my sister's apartment. I had moved in with one of my best friends to a cozy apartment in the West Village on Bedford Street. We could seat approximately five people between the love seat sofa (that pulled out into a single bed!), two bar stools, and a bean bag chair that made up our kitchen, living, *and* dining room area. Too proud to get a twin bed as an adult, my full-size bed took up my whole bedroom—if you can even call it a bedroom. Had it not been for a sliver of a window, it had likely been used as a walk-in closet for the previous tenant.

Seriously, if you turned to the side, you had to shimmy your way between the bed and the closet to access the closet. But I had my own closet! With my own clothes that fit me, not my sister. And we were living in an apartment where—rumor has it—Jimi Hendrix was a frequent visitor to our exact unit. His friend had occupied the space for decades before moving out. We heard that he might have died or moved into a nursing home—I hope it was the latter. Then the apartment was gut-renovated, and the exposed brick restored to its old glory. Here we were—two young, professional women—being asked to pay twelve times more a month than what this dude paid over the last fifty years. But we were having the time of our lives, and jaws would drop when we shared our address. It was all worth it.

Anyway, back to the annual plan presentation for the client meeting. It was August 23, 2011. Another warm and sticky summer day in NYC, for sure. But that didn't matter. No errands to Times Square on this day. I waited for our two-hour post-lunch meeting to begin all morning with butterflies in my stomach. I nervously opened up the presentation multiple times to internalize which slide came before mine so I would be prepared. What were my talking points? What was I going to say that was not on the slide? My palms remained sticky all morning, and my stomach churned endlessly. I kept telling myself to snap out of it! *I got this!* After all, this was just another stage performance where the performers were waiting to take their places before the lights went up. But that is normal for me. To this day, I still get those pre-presentation jitters that I've come to accept as nervous energy. It's the adrenaline boost I need to step out onto the stage—and quite honestly, I would now be lost without.

Finally, it was time. We entered a small conference room where the video chat was set up. Yes, we were video chatting via Skype for Business with our South Florida-based clients back in 2011. We were ahead of the times.

I had two slides in a deck of about fifty. I didn't care. They were *my* two slides. I couldn't wait to get to them and dive into the exciting data-based media relations plan we had put together for the coming year. I patiently waited my turn as my colleagues jumped back and forth doing the strategic set-up and sharing the meat of the plan.

I stole a beat to look around the room. I recognized that I was the youngest person in the room—and a young female at that. We also were presenting to an all-female team of clients. How cool was that! That euphoric feeling returned, and the butterflies subsided as my colleagues turned to me. My turn.

As I opened my mouth to speak and get going, I was thinking, *All good. I'm clear, confident.* I was genuinely excited. And then, about thirty seconds in, the building started to rumble.

Yes, our twenty-story, New York City skyscraper started rumbling. Then came the sound of sirens. I saw the look of panic amongst my team. No one knew what was happening, and in my mind, I couldn't help but think this might be a terrorist attack—I was so frightened!

At the same time, I was aware that our clients in South Florida were not experiencing what we were experiencing. I'd been conditioned to believe the show must go on. I had *no* clue what to do. So I decided to just keep going. The most senior member of the team left the room to find out what had happened midway through my presentation.

After what seemed like an eternity but was probably only sixty seconds later, our colleague returned and abruptly stopped me from blabbering on any further. She told us we'd just had an earthquake. She explained to the clients that we needed to pause, and of course, they fully understood. And then there was a moment where we all laughed—in the room and online virtually—at how I had powered through a presentation during what we later came to find out was a 5.8-magnitude earthquake. It had hit in Virginia and was felt all the way up to Boston. In the moment, the team looked at me in bewilderment that I had just kept going.

I realize now that sometimes we can be so focused on being somewhere or getting somewhere that we forget what really matters. It became a running joke amongst the team, but I still think about it from time to time. Was I a badass, or a bad teammate?

I work for a corporation now where our top priority is to "Put Safety

First." I was definitely not putting our safety first on that day. It almost seemed like common sense to have paused, but I was too concerned with messing up the presentation and wrecking our reputation with the senior client. I was concerned about losing the opportunity to be in the room again.

I realized later on that I was invited to be part of that conversation because I had earned a spot at the table and I wasn't going to lose the right to be there if I had paused to acknowledge that something scary was happening in our environment. In fact, that probably would've given me more credibility. But once again, you live and you learn. And now it makes for a great story!

Chapter 8

FINDING YOUR PURPOSE

L ess than a decade ago, the topic of "purpose"—for individuals, brands, and companies—became all the rage in the corporate world. Building brands with a purpose. Having a purpose-driven corporate culture. The list goes on. And while this suddenly became en vogue, you'll find no complaints from me on it.

I believe that having a strong sense of purpose can be an incredible energizer. It's a powerful tool, whether kept right in front of you on a daily basis, or lost and rediscovered at any point in time. There was only one problem: I hadn't defined my *own* purpose.

My first encounter with defining my personal purpose was an interesting one. One week before I was set to officially start work with my third employer in 2014, my soon-to-be manager suggested I join a leadership meeting outside the office focused on defining personal purpose. It was the second workshop of its kind that the company had given, with the first serving as a combination of defining personal and company purposes with the most senior leaders. Now the company wanted to open the exercise of defining personal purpose to a broader group of leaders.

I found this wildly fascinating and incredibly intimidating. Imagine this: you just agreed to join a new company, and you are days away from your official start. You join this workshop, where you are split into small groups and are supposed to work with these people to dig deep and uncover key moments of your life that helped define who you are. Then, taking all these moments that you have just unveiled to the person to your right—in my case, a complete stranger—you identify the red thread that runs throughout, ultimately coming up with a pithy statement that clearly defines your purpose. It's an incredible journey of self-reflection and discovery that enables you to tap into raw emotion and unearth milestone moments—the good and the bad—that shaped you.

People went all-in (as they should), taking the exercise seriously. My colleagues dug deep and shared accounts like the pain of losing a loved one or fighting through the diagnosis of a disease. They told heartwarming stories about the birth of a child and about that chance, humorous encounter that led to the meeting of a significant other. There were tears streaming. There were roars of laughter. Vulnerability was on everyone's sleeves. And I didn't know how to handle it. At the time, I chalked it up to being thrust into an uncomfortable and unfamiliar situation. I felt my young age like never before. At only twenty-six years old, I was the youngest one in the room amongst these leaders by at least three-to-five years. And remember, I had not even officially started at this company yet!

My group consisted of five friendly yet completely unfamiliar faces. On top of that, my group's facilitator was the head of the department I would be joining in a few short days. The pressure was on. Except it wasn't. I was the only one putting pressure on myself.

Looking back now, I realize it was my inability to be vulnerable that hindered my experience—not my lack of experience or my age. It shouldn't have mattered if these people were strangers or my closest friends. They were being vulnerable with me, opening up about life-changing moments, yet I couldn't break down the wall to truly be vulnerable with them. I was so focused on not making a fool of myself and coming up with a creatively worded purpose statement that I completely missed the point of the exercise. I wasted a tremendous opportunity.

And what ultimately ended up happening? I allowed those around me who listened to my surface-level stories define my purpose. I spoke about my love for acting yet how I always had that moment of nerves before I would go on stage. I mentioned that this followed me into my professional career. I love presenting, but there's always that pesky butterfly-in-the-stomach moment before I open my mouth.

We came up with a subpar statement that ripped off Taylor Swift's number one hit at the time, "Shake It Off." The statement was, "Shake it off and get on stage." It was a true statement that reflected a small piece of who I was at that moment in time but not my *purpose*. Simply put, we came up with a statement that reflected what I had put out, and nothing more. What else was I to expect?

I left that workshop doubting how things would work out with this company. I felt like a bit of a fool too—and in front of the most senior member of my new team! Truth be told, I also thought this company was slightly crazy for doing this. After all, back in 2014, the concept of purpose was just budding from a corporate perspective. I didn't quite get it, as I hadn't really encountered purpose-at-work yet. (Spoiler alert: I am now over eight years with that company, so things more than worked out.)

Three years later, in 2017, I had the opportunity to attend the next purpose workshop the company was giving to a new crop of leaders. I wasn't on the list since I had gone through one already, but when I caught wind of it, I gathered the courage to ask my boss if I could attend. I explained what had happened the first time and why I wanted another shot. She could've said no because I went through one already, or because I was leaving the US a month later to start an assignment abroad. But she said yes, and I was thankful she did.

This time, I went all-in. I tried to get the most out of the experience to make up for the last time. I remember walking away feeling much better but still not completely satisfied. Knowing that everyone would be asked to share their purpose at the end of the workshop, I was still so focused on creating that perfect statement that everyone would react to with a "yeah, that's you!" I was treating the exercise more like the creation of an ad campaign slogan, and a bad campaign at that, since I can't even recall what that statement was today. For someone who always has the words, I just couldn't come up with "the one."

It took years to realize the rich lessons here. Most obviously, I learned that no one can define your purpose for you, nor should you let them. It takes work to define your purpose, and it doesn't happen overnight. It doesn't need to be a pithy statement, and it doesn't need to resonate with anyone but you. But most importantly, I began to learn a very hard lesson on the importance of vulnerability.

Google "vulnerability in the workplace" and today you will find a plethora of resources.

The journey to define my purpose was one of those transformative experiences that also led me on my journey to understanding the importance of vulnerability in and outside the workplace. It took a good decade for me to be able to even name and understand that. Being more vulnerable is something I am just starting to scratch the surface of today.

Like so many young perfectionists, I had created a world in which vulnerability didn't exist. I spent many years questioning vulnerability in the workplace, and in my life, for that matter. For so long, what was put out into the world and played back to me was that women were emotional, and emotions at work were bad. Women were less than equal to men in the workplace, and just couldn't hack it like their male counterparts could. Men were the breadwinners. The all-too-familiar stereotypical list goes on.

When I set out in my professional career, I wanted one thing: to succeed. There was no room in my world for weakness or failure. And if it did happen, it was definitely not to be shared with the outside world—a far cry from what we see posted on the likes of LinkedIn by leaders today.

So, I strived to be that *always-can-make-it-happen, no-problems-here, can-do-it-all, kill-'em-with-kindness* type of a person. After all, my family called me "Dayna Sunshine"; I had a reputation to live up to.

And guess what? It worked. It worked for many years. Until it didn't anymore.

In fact, I once had a colleague call me out on it. She was my manager at the time, and we were at a team meeting outside the office. We were sitting on this beautiful estate in Southampton, New York and had broken out into one-on-one conversations in rotation with everyone on the team. We sat face-to-face, and I can't remember the question that prompted it, but my response was something along the lines of, "I feel like sometimes I can be two different people in my personal life and work life," and my then-manager looked me in the eyes and said, "But why?"

The bell to rotate to the next person was going to ding way before I could really get into that one, but the conversation stayed with me, and I kept her question in the back of my mind. I still do to this day. *"But why?"*

You get to a point in your career where it becomes less about you and your climb and more about others. Leading others. Managing others. Setting an example for others. Making that transition was not easy for me. I genuinely cared about others. I wanted others to succeed. I wanted the team I was on to succeed. But I also wanted to succeed. I wanted to succeed so badly that I became almost robotic in the workplace.

In the US, it is common to walk into the office in the morning, smile at others, and say almost simultaneously, "Good morning, how are you?" "Good, and you?" and keep walking.

"How are you?" has become a salutation, with no meaning behind it. A gesture of being collegial, and nothing more.

To my surprise, this was not the case in offices elsewhere. I remember distinctly an encounter about a year later with a colleague at the coffee machine at our company headquarters in Amsterdam. I didn't know this colleague too well at the time, so I smiled politely and said, "Hi, how are you?" I had no idea culturally this would be an invitation to launch into full-on conversation—I was expecting, whether good or bad, she would just give a polite nod and the ubiquitous, "Fine, thanks, how are you?" She *actually* told me how she was. After all, I did ask. It was way more than I had bargained for so early in the morning, and I couldn't understand it at first.

As a culture, the Dutch tend to be direct. You ask a question, they answer and tell it how it is. This is something I have grown to love and appreciate. However, what this made me realize was just how closed off I had become, and how unwilling I was to be vulnerable in even the most unassuming of situations. When did I go from that eighth-grader who enjoyed buttering and serving bagels at 7 a.m. on Friday mornings to someone who wanted to rush back to their desk to just get the job done? Where had the humanity in my daily interactions gone? And how could I regain the source of energy I used to get from speaking to people instead of having that same energy drained?

I started to notice how others acted and saw it wasn't just me. It was society around me. If someone asks, "How are you?" why do we defer to, "Fine, thanks. How are you?" instead of saying, "Doing well because today I am going to have a drink with a friend later who I haven't seen in a while" or "Rough morning—was running late and hurt my leg at the gym"?

The real revelation started to happen when I realized my lack of vulnerability in the workplace was being driven by my in ability to be vulnerable outside the workplace as well. And for me, it started with my inability to answer the simple question, "How are you?" in a truthful manner.

Being vulnerable—with my friends, family, and now with my colleagues—is something I had to relearn after I wrongly conditioned myself to check it at the door. I thought it was a sign of weakness instead of seeing it as a sign of power. Being in touch with how you are doing is powerful. And while it still doesn't always come naturally to me, I can tell you how freeing it feels when I am able to break through my own built-up wall.

I now recognize the moments when I am being vulnerable and can equally recognize the moments when I am holding back. Baby steps, but progress. And I think progress is always something worth celebrating.

While I was unable to define my purpose in 2014, and again in 2017, my moment finally did come. In spring 2021, I revisited the topic of purpose with a leadership and career coach who I was working with at the time. I was still focused on getting that perfect statement. I took our bimonthly call while out for a walk one day, meandering around Central Park. It was a beautiful early spring day, and after a brutal pandemic winter, I was in no rush to be back inside my 800-square-foot apartment.

My coach asked me a series of questions and had me fill out a sheet, which was essentially an exercise in writing my obituary. This sounds morbid, but it was a breakthrough exercise for me. I finally started to realize that my purpose was really something that needed to live within *me* and exist for *me*—not for others. This was when the walls of vulnerability started to come down.

I was finally satisfied. My quest had been fulfilled. I put a few words on a Post-It note and stuck it to my computer monitor, which served as a daily reminder of what I had written on the worksheet that helped quantify my purpose.

And then the strangest thing happened. Months later, I was sitting in my apartment thinking of my Papa. It was getting close to Thanksgiving time, eleven years since he had passed away. He had a heart aneurysm and miraculously held on for hours until my mom, my sister, and I got to Florida to say goodbye. I think of him all the time and feel his presence with me now.

This was the case when I went to bed that evening; I felt like he was guiding me. I was jolted out of sleep a few hours later. I sat straight up, and it came to me. This somewhat succinct statement captured what I would consider my purpose. So now I have it. I have my statement:

"To be the conductor of the orchestra who synthesizes all the notes to make the story sing!"

Chapter 9

RAISE YOUR HAND; YOU NEVER KNOW WHERE IT MIGHT LEAD

The purpose workshop in 2014 marked my first foray into the corporate world, and once I officially joined the company, I enjoyed my time there. For me, I knew my time working at creative agencies was meant to be intense training for what was my ultimate goal of working for a multinational corporation.

I joined the US subsidiary of one of the world's largest brewers and had a hybrid role handling internal and external communications on the corporate affairs team. This meant I could carry the external communications skills I had honed during my agency days into the corporate world, and also learn the realm of internal communications and employee engagement.

While I loved working for multiple clients as a consultant, by this point in time, I knew I wanted to be part of an actual business. When you're on the agency side, you're always limited to what the client gives you to work with and the limited background or context they provide. You spend many hours toiling over plans and working on projects that, once tossed over to the client, you never even know how they will be executed, or worse—whether they are executed, and what impact it has on the business. For me, it was crucial to one day make this type of a move, as I craved the opportunity to be part of—and make an impact within—a business.

My company had gotten involved with the Nudge Global Impact Challenge in Amsterdam the previous year, which was—back then—a three-day competition for young talents in the world of sustainability. The 2014 participant from my company was named one of three winners out of thirty talents from around the world. I admired this peer of mine, and I hung onto the stories she brought back. A few months later, the company put out a call again for those interested in participating in the 2015 Challenge.

In 2015, I was five whole years into my career, and although I was doing the job of someone with typically more years of experience, I was grateful my company had taken a chance on me. I was intrigued and wanted to participate, but I hesitated. After all, what do I know about sustainability? I recycled sometimes, and I thought more people should. I wasn't as wasteful as those around me. But let's be honest, I grew up surrounded by those who lived in the world of plenty, and even though the movie *An Inconvenient Truth* had come out several years earlier, the words "carbon footprint" and "CO2 emissions" were not yet in the average American or even New Yorker's vernacular. Sad, but true.

Something inside me told me to raise my hand. Maybe I would be selected. Maybe I would not. But you have to be in it to win it. I created a three-minute video on how the impacts of our nonsustainable practices are evident in today's society, and if we do not do our part to take action now, the world as we know it will soon change forever. I remember citing the government-mandated blackouts in Johannesburg and the impacts of global warming on our glaciers as examples. I submitted the video to the internal selection committee and hoped for the best.

A few weeks later, I received an email—I had been selected! Wow! I had been selected, and now I had no idea what I was going to do. My anxiety kicked in and stayed with me for several months as I went through that journey.

The first task was to identify a project to work on as part of the

Impact Plan that each participant would bring to Amsterdam. I came up with an idea that I thought was brilliant (I still do). I wanted to create the world's first recycling bar.

A *what*? A bar made of recycled goods?

Maybe, but also so much more! Here's how it would work: this bar would operate on the premise that in order to obtain a beer, you needed to recycle your old cans or bottles first. For example, a six-pack would be your currency for a pint. Of course, the bar would be heavily branded and stand in a booming New York City neighborhood for high visibility. After all, my marketing prowess and desire to tell a good story could be used for a good cause here, and I was not going to miss the opportunity to include that as part of the plan.

While in Amsterdam, we met with coaches and specialists to talk through our plans, get feedback, and help us take them to the next level. But ultimately, it was up to us to bring them to life. At the time, the heart of the program on-site would be three action-packed days of networking, team-building, working on leadership skills, listening to inspiring speakers, and working in groups. This was all part of a case competition that would help a real Dutch sustainable start-up come up with a tangible plan to help them achieve their objectives.

Everything we did was assessed, as we had assessors follow us around from activity to activity—watching and listening. The point of the assessors was to give you a full report post-Challenge that highlighted key strengths and areas for opportunity as a leader. When I was going through it, it was probably the most intimidating experience of my life thus far. But in the end, it was extremely helpful to get that kind of input. When else, really, do you come upon such candid feedback?

I met the most inspiring people. The guest speakers spoke about their own journeys and stories. I looked up in awe as Tony's Chocolonely Chief Chocolate Officer, Hank Jan Beltman, told the story of why Tony's was founded—in an effort to right the wrongs of the chocolate trade, which is laden with child labor and modern-day slavery. He explained how their business operates and I held on to every word. To this day, I feel pride in explaining to others why a bar of Tony's chocolate is not evenly portioned into perfectly even pieces like a Hershey or Cadbury bar.

Hint: It's to show the inequity in the world. How brilliant!

There I was—in another complete Forrest Gump moment—and I know what you may be thinking: *She's talking about chocolate again.* But what other way to describe this experience as selecting a piece from the box—hopefully a sustainably sourced chocolate box—biting into an unknown flavor, full of skepticism, and thinking you'll want to spit it out, only to realize you love it. And you want to know more about it. What is this flavor? Why have I never selected this one, or known about this before? Curiosity ensued, and the rest is history.

I took advantage of our coffee breaks to try to connect with as many participants as I could, and to get to know who these people were, where they came from, and what they did. As expected, most had impressive jobs in the world of sustainability, working for investment funds within major banks like ABN AMRO or municipalities and on the front lines of changing the game. I met sustainable fashion designers and consultants at global impact firms like Steward Redqueen. Everyone around me knew Steward Redqueen. Until that moment, I had not. I had only heard of consultancies like McKinsey, BCG, and Deloitte. And I thought consultancies worked on things like tackling financial-related corporate issues, not sustainability and impact. At the time, I never would've correlated company success with its sustainability agenda.

Here I was, a complete imposter in their world (or at least in my mind), who knew how to write a coherent press release and build a brand. I tried to keep my head high and muddle through.

Oh, and my plan? It got completely shat on. The experts around me asked really smart questions, but they just pointed out all the flaws:

"How do the bottles get to the recycling facilities?"

"What if you want another beer? Do you have to bring in another six-pack?"

"Are you adding additional carbon footprint with this setup versus just recycling the bottles in the normal system?"

"Is this hygienic?"

"Is this even legal in the United States given the three-tier distribution system?"

Forehead, meet palm of hand. My heart ached; my cheeks turned red. I felt defeated, but I had come so far (physically, at least). I was in this competition, and I was not going to give up.

The day came when we broke up into our small groups to work on our business plans for our assigned start-up. The challenge our entrepreneur gave us was to gain awareness of her company by highlighting what set it apart. It was a coffee company trying to create social change by fixing the inequitable coffee supply chain. Unlike big coffee chains, this company had a mission to leave its farmers, and the country where the product is produced, with more money in their pockets.

The task at hand: the company was relatively new and had little to no brand awareness. They existed—and for a good cause—but sales were slow because they were an unknown entity. We were challenged to come up with a campaign that would bring brand awareness by touting the brilliant differentiating factor this company possessed from its competition—*I could do this!* No one else in my group had a marketing/comms background. My red-faced cheeks faded into delightful glee as I started to lead the group by guiding them through what we needed to do. In simple terms, I explained how I thought we needed to get more insight into who the target audience was and where we could intersect them. "With the limited budget we have, how can we also extend our presence using other forms of amplification—like the news and social media versus paying for traditional advertising like TV ads or billboards?" There were head nods around the room as we divided up the group to work on different aspects of building the campaign. Soon we were writing on whiteboards, mapping out plans, all working together to bring our unique strengths to the table.

We found out that many of the client's customer base were frequent travelers who often stopped at the airport in Dubai to get from the east to west (and vice versa), and what better place than an airport to gain access to a captive audience (delayed flights, long layovers, etc.)?

Our plan centered around a pop-up experience in the airport to introduce consumers to the brand and educate them about the product and the company mission so that when they arrived back home in their respective European markets, they would be inclined to seek out the brand. We spoke about the type of earned media potential this idea could have, how we could leverage social media, and how many potential consumers we would reach based on the position of the pop-up in the airport terminal. It was a complete home run! Our group was named the winner of that portion of the challenge.

With my spirits slightly lifted, I went into day three with an open mind. That afternoon, we were to find out who the top participants were based on ratings from a number of factors thus far: participation in the different group activities, comments from the assessors, peer comments, and how your group fared in the case competition. These final ten participants would give a speech illustrating the reasons why they should be one of the final three winners. My expectations were low. At this point, I was just happy to be in Amsterdam and to have met such cool people.

And then came time for the announcement of the ten finalists. One-by-one, I listened and cheered along with my peers for these remarkable young leaders. The last name was called . . . and it was me! I was shocked. Truly. Well, this was fantastic, beyond fantastic actually. *But what the heck would I do now? And would this be "the moment" where I am found out for not being as much of an expert in the sustainability space as my peers?*

I had about two minutes to vie for my spot as one of the final three. How would I approach this? I knew what my weaknesses were, but what were my strengths? I ultimately chose candor, and I chose to do what I liked to do best: tell a story.

I sat in a booth outside of our plenary room in the late afternoon. It was November, and the sun was nearly set in the Netherlands. I remember feeling a cold chill from the room as my sweaty palm clutched the Nudge Challenge branded pen. I wrote ferociously. I didn't have a lot of time to prepare. I scribbled notes—bullet points and key messages to get across. I thought about my setup. How would I be able to evoke something from everyone sitting in that room? The pen dropped with a few moments to spare. I reread my notes, took a breath, and waited as the other nine participants stood up before me to give their pitches.

My heart raced and I half-listened to what they said. In reality, I didn't listen at all. Finally, it was my turn. I held on tight to my notebook and approached the podium, took a breath, and I told my story.

"Close your eyes," I began. "No, seriously! Please close your eyes." I waited a beat. And then I started again.

I asked the group to put themselves in my shoes. I told them to travel back to three days ago, and to picture themselves arriving in a foreign country and a competition where you realize you don't belong and don't have the knowledge that everyone around you has. And then I told the rest of my story. How I felt over the last three days—the highs and lows. Being knocked down over my plan and built back up over the case competition work with my team. I spoke about feeling inadequate for three days straight and also the desire to learn as much as I could and make new friends. It was raw, open, and honest. It felt oddly satisfying to bare my soul to this group of international strangers. It was emotional. My voice was a little shaky, but my confidence started to build as I went on. I took a breath when I was done. Another beat. There was silence. I told everyone to open their eyes. And then they started to applaud. I smiled. I felt relieved, accomplished, and satisfied. I was less shaky on the walk back to my seat than on the walk to the podium just moments before, and I had a proud smile on my face.

I bet you're thinking here is where I say, "And guess what, I WON!" Except I didn't. I didn't make it into the final three, but by being in the top ten, I was closer than I'd ever imagined I could've been three days earlier. And while you may also be thinking the lesson here was "winning isn't everything," it was so much more than that.

The lesson for me was to "take risks." To raise my hand, even when

I don't necessarily know the answer. To put myself out there. You never know what might be waiting on the other side if you don't.

I also learned, during this time, to listen, and I mean, really listen to feedback. It was a masterclass in self-awareness. I recognized some of the feedback that I saw in the assessor's post-Challenge recap. And then there was some feedback I didn't recognize as being "me."

Self-awareness is an important skill, and I use the word "skill" purposefully. There is a natural, innate ability to be self-aware, and then there is learned self-awareness. Up until that point, I functioned only on the innate self-awareness. I just didn't think about it, or really know I should think about it, as actively as I do now. That's a key learning in itself!

My experience at Nudge changed my career trajectory. A few months after I participated in the competition, our US head of Corporate Social Responsibility was leaving to go back to the global team in Amsterdam. I approached my boss at the time, fully admitting I was no expert (even though she clearly already knew that), and using the confidence I had gained at Nudge, I put my hand up to take her job. To my surprise, I was afforded the opportunity, and I set off on an ambitious journey to rewrite the US strategy for our environmental, social, and responsible consumption agenda.

As part of my job, I joined the board of the newly formed Glass Recycling Coalition, and was an active participant in the member meetings of The Recycling Partnership. I listened more widely than ever before. More often than not, I felt like an idiot. I read a lot. I asked questions, although admittedly not enough. I learned something new every day. I created a plan and reshaped the agenda. I never felt more challenged and, therefore, accomplished in my life.

Nudge and its impact stay with me each and every day. In fact, I was invited to be a peer keynote speaker to help kick off the 2018 Challenge. The program has become so much bigger than it was back then, with over ninety participants taking part in any given year. I currently serve as a peer guide and mentor to current participants. I am inspired every time I speak to my group. The work they are doing is going to change the world. They give me energy and hope, but most importantly, they remind me that "imposter syndrome" is all in our heads.

After all, as Walt Disney once said, "If you can dream it, you can be it."

It would be remiss of me not to share one more anecdote from my first Nudge experience. One of the recommended readings coming from my assessors was the book *Nice Girls Don't Get the Corner Office.* The second I saw the title on the page, I resented the book *and* the recommendation. I strongly believe then, as I do now, that nice girls *can* get the corner office.

I did, of course, go on to read the book, and it was part of the impetus for me to write my own story. While I don't disagree with some of the overarching tips in the book, I still resent the title.

As someone who strongly believes one size does not fit all, I felt at the time that the book was trying to tell me that by following those exact prescribed steps and actions, I could get the corner office one day, and if I strayed from that path, I could forget about it.

This might sound ironic coming from me. The thing is, you can advise, guide, and coach all you want, but until people make their own mistakes and are able to identify and name their own learnings, nothing said in those kinds of books—including my own story—will sink in.

I also truly believe nice women *can and do* land up in corner offices. I've seen it happen multiple times. Being nice, or too nice, is not what's stopping women from rising. It's when you begin to go against who you are and try to be someone you think you are supposed to be instead of your authentic self that the corner office will become further away from your reach.

Chapter 10

THE YOUNGEST ONE IN THE ROOM AND THE ONLY FEMALE

W hen my sister left New York to go to school in Chapel Hill, North Carolina, there were some in our community who were surprised. "Nice, Jewish girls don't go *there*." The same comment reared its ugly head when I decided to follow her there three years later.

I like to defy stereotypes. That is why, when I joined the beer industry and started hearing, "Nice Jewish girls don't work there," or even better—this time from a soon-to-be former colleague at the company I was leaving—"Why would you go there? You're going to get a beer belly," I rolled my eyes, blocked out the noise, and continued on.

This time, unfortunately, those naysayers were (somewhat) right. But religion and beer bellies had nothing to do with it. The alcohol industry, unsurprisingly, is a historically male-dominated industry. I was fortunate, though, to join a company that employed many fantastic women, some of whom held very senior positions. At the time, there were two incredible women on the management team. This pulled a bit of a shade over my eyes in my day-to-day when it came to the lack of female representation in the industry, but all that changed when I attended my first industry event.

It was the fall of 2014. I was twenty-six years old and had been with the company for just about six months at this point. I was a strong, independent female, making a pretty acceptable salary and living on my own—without a roommate—in New York City. This, in itself, was considered to be quite a feat.

At this point, I had spent five years consistently being the youngest one in the room. I recognized it, appreciated it, was becoming a bit used to it, and it took more these days to shake my confidence in these situations (even if the pre-presentation butterflies remained). I wasn't easily intimidated by being the youngest or being female anymore. On the contrary, I was proud. And I hoped that I represented well.

There's always that moment that gets you, though.

I had traveled halfway across the country to the annual National Beer Wholesalers Association meeting in New Orleans. It was a long day of travel and catching up on work, and now there was a kick-off happy hour. I changed into a more suitable outfit for the occasion—a Banana Republic suit dress that just so happened to be the color of my employer's iconic bottle, and a pair of patent leather, nude Kate Spade heels—and made my way to the reception. As I turned left and opened the door to the courtyard, I immediately froze. In those days, I hadn't yet succumbed to contact lenses, and I often went without my glasses because I was convinced I didn't need them as much as I did. I could get by when walking around Manhattan because I knew my way around. The squinting for street signs wasn't an issue until I wandered into a new neighborhood. But the truth was, my distance vision was pretty bad *and* getting worse!

To enter the courtyard, I'd have to travel down a steep set of stairs, and I could already tell all eyes were on me because not only was I about to be one of approximately five women in the room, I was the youngest by at least ten years.

It was humid, and I was sweating. I couldn't make out any faces because, as already established, I didn't have my glasses on. It's amazing though, because I really didn't need my glasses to see that 98.5 percent of the faces staring at me belonged to white, middle-aged men. There were lots of khaki pants and blue blazers. A lot of salt and pepper hair. I could've felt like Cinderella entering the ball, but instead, I felt like a piece of meat arriving via a pole at a strip club.

As if that wasn't bad enough, I had to first make it down the stairs without falling in my heels, which were now clinging to my sweaty and swollen feet due to the humidity and travel. Then, I had to find the group comprising my colleagues amidst the crowd while squinting.

I clutched the rail as I gritted my teeth, breathed heavily through my nose, and tried to ignore the sweat exuding from every pore of my body.

I eventually found my (all-male) colleagues who graciously took me into their circle and included me in the conversation as if I was one of them. Because I *was* one of them. They didn't pay attention to my gender. I was never made to feel like I didn't belong or like they wanted me there for another reason. I recognize how lucky I had been at the time, and how unfortunately rare it is. I have heard too many stories at other places where that has not been the case, and it truly makes me sick.

It was definitely a moment I will never forget, and unfortunately it wouldn't be the last time I'd find myself in a situation like that. Many females make light of it—after all, there are never any lines for the ladies' rooms at industry events. This is, however, a problem we must work on addressing and changing. There are many who are doing so, including my current employer. But we still have a long way to go as an industry.

What did I learn? In that moment, I learned many things. First off, to breathe. A deep breath can help you reset, especially in the most stressful of moments. I learned to make a decision and stick with it. My decision was to be myself and to not let the fear of being a fish out of water come over me. Why should I cower in the corner? Why should I go back to my hotel room and spend the evening alone? I had every right to be there, and I was there as an equal, not as someone's daughter or a Vegas showgirl.

I also learned to listen to my body, which had been telling me for a while my vision was getting worse, and now it needed to be addressed.

I learned how to turn a conversation so I could partake. When I joined my colleagues, they were talking about football (the American kind). Talk about stereotypes! It's a sport I don't care much for. College basketball, on the other hand, that's one I can contribute to, so I slowly turned the conversation and soon we were talking about one of the greatest college rivalries of all time: UNC and Duke. A topic I know pretty well. Go Heels!

Lastly, it was at that moment that I knew I wanted to be part of a movement to make change and contribute to creating a more diverse work environment. An opportunity came soon after with a seat on our Women's Leadership Forum board, but it wouldn't be until years later that I would get to work on the company's first ever corporate communications campaign that would focus specifically on gender diversity in the alcohol beverage industry. And when the going got tough on the journey to strategize, sell-in, and execute that campaign, I consistently traveled back to this exact moment to remind myself how important this work was not only to me, but to so many others. It became clear that there was only one way to go from here, and that was to keep marching forward.

Chapter 11

UNLEASHING THE VELVET HAMMER

T he first time my boss called me "the Velvet Hammer" was sometime around August 2014. I never heard the term before, so sheepishly, I accepted the name and turned to Google for help.

Urban Dictionary, the most valid source in the world, was quick to answer the call:

The Velvet Hammer is a woman leader or professor who can manage with grace and eloquence and still get things done. She is very tough on her underlings, but fair and brilliant. She is also very beautiful and probably will save/rule the world one day.

Okay. Thanks? I could get behind this. I think.

The project that earned me the honor was our annual employee meeting, one of the main projects I would manage in my first role—communications and events manager—at my current employer. This was the internal communications part of that hybrid external/internal communications job referenced earlier. Managing a meeting of the sort was both a source of professional growth and personal anxiety.

Prior to this project, I also took for granted what goes into an internal gathering for employees—whether it be a two-hour town hall or a multiple-day event. Every detail is thought of—from the timing of the agenda to the inspirational theme—and there needs to be a strategic storyline to serve as the red thread woven throughout the event to achieve the event's objectives. Of course, no matter how much planning goes on behind the scenes, the only thing people will remember is if the chicken was cold at lunch or the lines in the bathroom were too long. Human nature, I suppose.

As a relatively new member of the company, I was in charge of project managing others from the business who had been around the employee meeting block and had no time to teach me along the way. Luckily, I did have an amazing colleague who managed the program previously and was an incredible source of help and partner in crime.

I was in charge of all the content *and* logistics. I quickly learned through this experience that I am not an events person, as I couldn't care less about what kind of protein is served for lunch. I am, however, very much into content and making sense of several different (and often complex) storylines to tell one cohesive, overarching story that motivates and inspires 500+ of my closest colleagues.

Unfortunately for me, logistics came with the gig. So, I'd focus my daytime hours on content in the boardroom with the management team and the evening hours responding to emails about menus, after-party logistics (*more* menus), and my all-time favorite (said no one, *ever*): transportation! Why was moving people from point A to point B so damn complex and time-consuming?!

I leaned into this experience as I would any other challenge—with an open mind—as I took note of what I liked *and* what I didn't like. Every time I wanted to cry when someone asked me to approve another food menu or look at signage for the walls of the event space, I tried to remember to take a breath and think of the bigger picture. I had direct access to our management team. Some people will never get this kind of access, and here I was on day one, waltzing right into the boardroom.

In a series of what would become "youngest one in the room" moments for the project, I spent my first twelve weeks at the company working alongside our management team and learning the ins and outs of the business from sales leaders as they helped me shape the program. It was a crash course in executive management and our business. I couldn't have asked for a better way to start off than to be thrown into the deep end of this specific project pool.

I didn't know at the time but this would turn out to be one of those career-defining moments that, although it came with tons of angst when it came to designing food menus, ended up helping me launch my career at my company. Why? Because I learned to make the time in front of these executives count. I went back to my earlier-in-career client-meeting days—I remembered to listen, to be prepared to share my opinion, and to not make anyone regret giving me the chance to have a seat at the big kids' table. I also got to know our most senior company executives in the US, some of whom have gone on to lead the global organization today.

As always, I was acutely aware of my age in these meetings. Here I was—twenty-six years old and recently plucked from the PR consultancy world into a major corporation—sitting at an oversized boardroom table in a big conference room with all the bigwigs. Those people with the C's in front of their titles. And they were listening to *me!* Following *my* recommendations, *my* agenda, and *my* overall guidance! When the conversation would switch between the topic at hand and other business, sometimes they would turn to me and ask for *my* opinion. I wasn't treated just as the "employee meeting update girl," I was treated as a colleague with a voice.

Nana (my grandmother) just couldn't believe it. In fact, completely unsure of what I did, she went around telling everyone who would listen in her senior community in South Florida that I was pretty much the CEO of my company. I was her little girl in big business!

The event came and went and was voted as one of the strongest in recent years amongst employees. As the wrap-up reports and post-mortems were conducted, I started to understand my boss's meaning of "the Velvet Hammer" as it pertained to me.

Simply put, it was a style of managing up, across, and down by holding tight to my nice girl persona while still effectively influencing and "getting sh*t done on time and in full," as they say in the corporate world.

But it wasn't an act. I was just me being me. That is who I was, who I have always been, and who I continue to be. And this is why I know a nice girl like me *can* one day get the corner office.

❊

Having a seat at the table during my employee meeting days only fueled my ambition to grow within the company and to perfect the state of being the Velvet Hammer. I have always been ambitious. I blame my curiosity and desire to learn for that.

I believe there are two types of ambitious people: ambitious planners who like to have a roadmap on how to get from A to Z in their careers, and ambitious pantsers who want to reach the top but have no qualms about the journey they will go on to get there.

For many years, I was the former. And for such ambitious planner types, ambition can sometimes be overwhelming, especially when you get stuck on the way from A to Z.

There's one conversation I can vividly recall that set the ambitious planner in me into full-on panic mode. I've never been one to get intimidated, especially by older, more senior men, but it does happen, and when it does, it really rattles me.

I was sitting in a large conference room with the global head of our function who was visiting the team from Europe. The observer in me took note of the room from the moment I walked in for our one-on-one conversation. It seemed like an odd choice. Of course, as the visitor, he did not pick this room. The room was meant for a group, not an intimate conversation, but because there were only two of us, you felt swallowed up by its size and the distance between the two parties. It was late afternoon and gray. The sun had never really risen that day, but with dusk upon us, you knew it was not going to make an appearance now.

My interactions with this executive thus far during my time at the company had been limited. In fact, this was likely the first time we had ever interacted. My boss had set up individual meetings with him and each member of the team. It was my turn.

After the brief introductions, he looked at me square in the eye and got straight to the point. He said, "What is your ambition?"

And I looked back at him square in the eye and confidently said, "One day, I want your job."

Good one, I thought. Strong, confident, even a little bold.

And I wasn't lying. That is, at least at the time, what I wanted.

And what he did next was a favor. He told me how to get there.

He asked me a simple question in return. "Who do you know?"

Usually quick and smooth on my feet, I stumbled. "Who do I *know*? What do you mean?"

He launched into what I now recognize as advice: "You need to know people. Recruiters. Peers at other corporations. Members of government. Leaders at non-governmental organizations (NGOs)."

Maybe he misunderstood me. He must've misunderstood me. I wanted *his* job, at *this* company. In the distant future, of course. I was going to work very hard, and I was going to get it one day. I knew the management team in the US quite well by then from my employee meeting experience and subsequent projects. Why would I need to know *other* people?

As I sat with the silence for a moment—an incredibly hard thing for me to do—my confidence in my assumptions began to wane. I think I even started to choke up a bit when I internalized his question: "Who do you know?"

I had worked with one recruiter who recruited me away from my first job to join my second company. For job no. 3, at this current company, an old colleague reached out with the job. So, I knew her. But at that stage in my career, I didn't really *know* anyone.

I remember feeling intimidated, overwhelmed, and somewhat humiliated, although that was definitely *not* the intention of his question or the conversation. I left the meeting thinking I had most certainly made a poor impression, and therefore, my future at this company—and maybe all others—was likely limited. Maybe I wasn't capable of becoming a chief corporate affairs officer for a multinational corporation like he was. Maybe I was only meant to be the Velvet Hammer who led cross-functional projects and just got the job done.

It took years to appreciate the advice I had been given. I didn't forget it, but I recognized I needed to compartmentalize it, so I placed it somewhere it wouldn't halt my underlying ambition and let it linger over the years: "Who do you know?"

As I reflect on this moment, about seven years later, I now know what he meant. I think back to how young and inexperienced I was. He could've clarified further. He could've said, "Do your job, and do it well. With time, your network will grow. You will come to know many people." But he didn't. He left me with the stillness and ambiguity, and I had to do the work myself. I recognize this now as a gift. At the time, it was disabling, but now it is empowering.

Everywhere I go, I meet people. Maybe I will never interact with these people again, maybe I will. LinkedIn has helped me keep track of these interactions and turn them into ongoing connections—it helps me manage my network even when the initial interaction is long behind us.

Every now and then, an update or post from one of these connections will catch my eye. I'm never ashamed to like or comment—or, if merited, send a direct message—even if we haven't spoken in several years. This is what staying connected is all about.

It's amazing to see colleagues I've worked with grow in their careers, and when I catch their promotion posts on LinkedIn, why wouldn't I want to celebrate them? It's even more gratifying seeing former interns and direct reports grow in their careers!

And the ultimate kicker in all of this for me is that keeping up a network of "people you know" is made easier when you are *nice* to people. People remember nice people, and they also remember not-so-nice people. People want to help nice people. People are rooting for nice people as they grow in their careers.

On top of being a nice person, I've learned you have to be an open and authentic person. I don't mean you need to be willing to reveal your life story to someone you just met. I find people can really tell the difference when you're open to truly connecting and when you're treating the interaction as a duty. It doesn't take much to be genuine and go beyond the standard name plus title introduction in a first encounter, and you never know where this new connection may lead. In my opinion, there's always more potential upside to making a new connection than down.

This is also key for me to be able to retain my Velvet Hammer status—to be able to grow your network and build influence is key to getting things done. Although there was a time in my life when I was unfamiliar with the phrase, once someone gives you the title, you don't want to give it up!

At a certain point in my career, recruiters started finding me—via LinkedIn and email. It was a somewhat euphoric turning point. I was wanted—or could be wanted—outside of where I currently was. But for me, there was just one problem—I wasn't looking to go anywhere. I already felt wanted, and I was satisfied with my job.

I came to realize that taking calls from recruiters was not a bad thing—it's not devious or disloyal. There may come a day when I feel it is time to go because opportunities have dried up, or my company tells me it's time to go. Or there may come a day when I am recruiting for my team, or a friend finds themself out of a job and needs support—or beyond recruitment, I need to partner with someone on something or need advice. And when any of those days come, I need to be ready. I need to know people.

Over the years I have built my network to where I can confidently say I know people now, but I also know there are still so many people to get to know along my journey. I am nowhere near obtaining the job level this executive from Europe held back then, nor do I know as many people as he did, but I am much closer than I was. And aside from just knowing people, I can say I have genuinely built relationships with people all over the world—and that has to be one of the most gratifying realizations.

Chapter 12

LEARNING TO TAKE CARE OF MYSELF AND OTHERS

When we were children and we were sick, we stayed home from school. Usually, we went to the doctor *and* stayed home from school. And if we were super lucky, we were back from the doctor in time to watch *The Price is Right* at 11 a.m. Any other Bob Barker fans out there?

Why is it then that when we're sick as adults, sick days no longer seem to exist?

If you ask most adults, they are more than likely to say that taking a sick day is looked down upon and/or there's just too much work to do to not show up. Both are issues in their own right, but the latter is what I want to zoom in on.

For many years, I was the worst anti-sick-day offender. What I've come to realize is that sometimes many of us—me included—send ourselves down our own rabbit hole, thinking the team cannot function without us. Nine and a half times out of ten, that is absolutely false. What I realized at some point was that I really needed to get over myself and focus on taking better care of myself.

From 2014 to 2016, I was always on the road. There was always somewhere to be and somewhere to go. I loved living life like George Clooney in *Up in the Air*. After all, wasn't this the time in my life to be doing this?

In 2015, there was an endless circuit of travel between New York, Los Angeles, New Orleans, and back. Every five to six weeks, I would come down with crippling tonsilitis. I'll spare you the details, but it was the "can't really talk or swallow" kind.

This went on throughout the year. The doctor couldn't figure out what was wrong. My medicine cabinet looked like a pharmacy, and on one of the last visits, the doctor said the next time this happened, we had to make plans for removing my tonsils. I freaked out because, at the ripe old age of twenty-seven, I knew getting your tonsils out after your teenage years was ill-advised and a major production. I was also taken back instantly to when I needed to have two of my wisdom teeth removed.

It was back in 2010, and I was in my first agency job. Not only was the procedure excruciatingly painful for me, but my jaw locked after the procedure, and I had trouble opening my mouth for about ten days. When you can't open your mouth, you cannot do certain things—like eat or brush your teeth. At a certain point, I had to return to the office. There was one day when a client was having an issue and everyone more senior on the team was traveling. I distinctly remember the managing director came over to me to ask my opinion on something related to the issue, and I had to tell her not to come closer as I covered my foul-smelling, unbrushed teeth that also reeked from the bits of chocolate pudding I tried to fling into my mouth as I withered away from hunger. The moral of this story was, I should've stayed home until I could open my mouth.

One day, a few months into the ongoing tonsil saga, I was lying in my bed at home, fever raging, tonsils the size of golf balls, and pounding Halls lozenges as if I were a chain smoker and these were my cigarettes. During these episodes, I didn't dare go into the office—first of all, the commute was over an hour away, and second of all, while I may have been a workaholic, I always found it disgusting to see people with a cough, cold, or some kind of obvious illness potentially spreading their germs around the office. And this was pre-COVID-19!

Although I have high standards when it comes to preventing the spread of germs, I was no saint in this regard. In fact, I viewed these as work-from-home days instead of rest-and-get-better days, which was partially why I was never getting better.

Anyway, during this one particular day, we were getting close to the launch of a big, important project that I was leading. Of course I was going to join the 2 p.m. status call. Who else was going to lead this thing? And besides, this was way too important. My health could take a backseat. I'd get a good night's sleep later and hopefully be back in the office as soon as possible.

Not only did my boss join the call, because she knew I was sick again and was going to cover for me, but my boss's boss also joined the call. When they saw I was online, they were NOT happy. I vividly remember hearing some stern words that may have included a threat to lock me out of my email account.

Touché.

For whatever reason, that was the wake-up call I finally needed to learn my lesson when it came to work and illness. I jumped off the call and went back to bed for the rest of the day.

It sounds obvious, but that year I learned that your health is not something to be taken for granted. I learned that missing a day or even several days because you are really sick (or on vacation) is okay. A company that has been around for over 150 years is not going to go under because Dayna Adelman did not show up to work that day.

I also decided, after that incident, that I should probably seek out a second opinion from another doctor the next time my tonsils flared up. Low and behold, I shared the cocktail of drugs I had previously been given and Doc No. 2 rolled his eyes. He said, "Try this," and handed me a prescription for something else. He said that if this didn't work, then we could consider surgery, but he was pretty confident he wouldn't be hearing from me again.

I like to think the medicine he prescribed was about one-third of the cure. From that day forward, I decided it was time to really put my health first. It was also high time I started paying attention to what I put in my body, and I really needed to start moving more. I sought out a local trainer at the gym and thus began my commitment to regularly exercising several times a week. I hadn't been inside a gym since college, and I hadn't gone for a run since I was forced to run a timed mile during preseason soccer training in high school. It was time.

That medicine, my trainer, prioritizing sleep, and my change in outlook saved me. I was feeling worn out at twenty-seven because I wasn't being kind to my body, and all because I couldn't get over myself in the workplace. The number of sick days I've had to take since this incident ironically (or not) have been minimal because I've been healthier over the last few years than I had been my whole life. However, I am now the biggest proponent of the adult sick day, although admittedly, it is not the same without Bob Barker hosting *The Price is Right*.

❀

I needed to learn how to take care of myself because I knew I wanted to take care of others one day. I had been "leading" my whole life—from the days on the student council to the soccer field and all the leadership trainings I was selected for. Yet, as I kept growing in my career, I yearned for a real direct report or team of my own to manage.

When I took on the role of leading Corporate Social Responsibility—now called Sustainable Development—in 2016, the opportunity came with my first ever real direct report. Sure, I had managed interns and junior colleagues on the agency side before, but with so many levels above me in those days, I was never really tasked with more than day-to-day executional management.

This was my first foray into becoming a boss, and the opportunity was both extremely exhilarating and incredibly daunting. This was particularly the case, as I was moving into a role where I'd have to manage a colleague of mine who had also become a friend. We had started days apart from each other in spring 2014 and learned the rules of the road at the company together. We commuted together and confided in each other. This colleague was a complete subject matter expert in the world of sustainability, whereas I was simply a high-performer who was given an amazing professional growth opportunity.

I knew it would only be a matter of time until this colleague chose to leave the organization, but I was determined to make our time together meaningful for both of us. I approached our working relationship like a true partnership. After all, I really valued what she brought to the table. While she may have been the subject matter expert, I brought other benefits to the relationship, such as being able to navigate the business (namely, the politics) and to drum up the support and buy-in we needed from many internal parties to bring our agenda to life. I like to think we worked well together. I also think we accomplished a lot together in terms of reshaping our agenda and achieving many "firsts" in a relatively short amount of time.

As to be expected, she resigned about four months later.

When it came time to hire for the open role, I agreed with my colleague who ran the government affairs side of the team that the needs of the team were changing and we would reframe this person's scope to be split between both agendas. In doing so, I knew this meant ending up with a direct report who was not going to be based in New York, but most likely with my colleague in Washington, DC. I had been managed over the years from afar by bosses based on the West Coast but had never managed anyone who wasn't right next to me.

Managing from afar proved to be a challenge. I struggled to get to really know this colleague and integrate them into the business, since the corporate teams all sat in New York, and our DC office was an office of two.

I learned many valuable lessons from this period of time that would come into play years later when I would find myself managing a direct report again—remote or non-remote:

- Picking up the phone is always better than emailing or messaging; you can't tell tone or intent over email.

- It's better to over-invest than under-invest, to set things off on the right track even if you don't have the time. Newsflash: you'll never have the time!

- There's more to work than the actual work; managing means getting to know people and what makes them tick. What are their drivers? What do they want out of this relationship? What do they want out of their careers?

- You get back what you put in; it takes time to build a strong relationship with a direct report (see above bullet!).

- Everyone needs to be managed differently! Sometimes being more hands-on is necessary and sometimes it is not.

- Sometimes people work best with lots of autonomy, and sometimes people are not autonomous at all but won't ask for help—it is up to you to identify where the team member sits on the spectrum and flex to their needs rather than carrying on and forcing your own upon him or her.

When I eventually moved on from this role, I knew one thing: I still had a lot to learn when it came to mastering the art of being a boss, but it was something I surprisingly enjoyed. This was a major factor that would eventually weigh heavily into my career decisions down the road. This was because I also started to realize that being a manager is not always a given as you progress in your career, especially in the corporate world, where structures remain very flat.

I knew that in order to reach my long-term goals and become the professional I wanted to be, it was important for me to continue to gain proper people-management experience. If I wanted to be an empathetic leader, it was going to take hands-on practice. If I wanted to help develop and grow someone in their own career path, it was going to take hands-on practice. If I wanted to create a high-performing team, it was going to take hands-on practice. And it was also going to take time. This likely wasn't going to happen in a quarter, half, or even one year, as I had done everything else. Managing someone—or a team—was going to be a longer-term time investment.

Many people choose to go the siloed route, and that's okay. I do think it is important to recognize which kind of professional you want to be. If it's the type who wants to manage a team and help people grow, it is really important to make sure you are finding ways to get that experience. There's nothing worse than becoming the boss one day because you're promoted based solely on your own performance-based merits and only then learning how to be a manager when you're pretty high at the top. I've seen that backfire several times, and it is so unfair not only to the individual but, more importantly, to their team.

Chapter 13

START WITH THE END
IN MIND

In the fall of 2007, my friend and I sat on my twin XL dorm room bed in Granville Towers at UNC at Chapel Hill with a smattering of brochures laid out on study abroad programs. We knew we both wanted to go to London, and we also knew we wanted to go together. However, that's where our shared ambitions ended—she wanted to do an internship program, and I wanted a more traditional study program. To me, it seemed asinine to pay to do free work, as you still needed to pay the school the semester of tuition to take part in the program. But in the end, her logic won over, and we were off to London the next fall. It was the best decision I ever made (well, she technically made for me).

During my (unpaid) internship, I got to work at a multinational corporation in what I considered to be the "new" center of the universe. Up until that point, New York City held that designation in my mind. However, when I got to London, I realized how diverse and international the city was—inside and outside the office. It was during this experience that I knew, somehow, some way, I would find my way back to Europe to work in my postgraduate years.

That opportunity came in the winter of 2017, when I had the chance to join the Global Communications team at my company's headquarters in Amsterdam. I couldn't believe it—although I could—because I had done everything in my power to position myself in a way so that when an opportunity like this arose, I would be top of mind with the right people.

From my first interview with the company back in 2014, I was very open about what intrigued me about the company and my long-term goals. In fact, if someone is going to ask you where you see yourself in five years, you might as well tell them the truth.

I loved that this company operated in over eighty countries around the world, which I took to mean there was room to grow and expand with the company quite literally anywhere. Because I never hid my ambition to work for the company abroad, it was baked into my personal development plan from day one. I took every opportunity I could to network—when I went to Amsterdam for the Nudge competition, I spent a day in the office and set up meetings with the Global Communications team. When I joined one of the annual function meetings in Italy, I tried to meet as many colleagues from around the world as I could. When I went on a personal trip to London, I stopped into the office and met with the team in the UK. This didn't mean I was gunning to leave the US when I first joined in 2014. Not at all. I loved my job, and I loved my team. It just meant that when the time was right and when the right opportunity came along—both for myself and the company—I might be in a better position to step into it.

Starting with the end in mind, or working backward from the goal, is a technique that was also engrained in me during my time at Nudge. Taking on a major project—or impact plan with the end-goal of making substantial change in the world—can be daunting. However, if you have an end-goal and can put that on paper and then break it up—month-by-month, little-by-little—you can work backward. This type of planning somehow makes it more manageable to reach your endpoint.

In October 2016, at a meeting in Amsterdam, I vividly remember having a conversation with the global director of communications. There was to be a position on his team in the coming months, and he wanted to gauge my interest. He walked me through the opportunity in full—the good, the bad, and some of the ugly. I appreciated his honesty, but most of all, I greatly appreciated that he was considering me. I had to try hard not to squeal with excitement. It was a joyous moment that was met with so many emotions, namely a sense of accomplishment, and then nerves.

My sense of accomplishment came from achieving that dream I set out for myself after my internship in London. My eyes had forever been opened to the prospects of living and working abroad at a young age and being able to fulfill that prophesy only seven years after setting the goal and still being somewhat young in my own career was extremely satisfying.

I spent the next day walking around Amsterdam seeing the city from a completely different perspective. Could I see myself living here? It was my fourth time in the city—the first two times had been for leisure (once with friends and once with my mom—two very different experiences), and the second two times for work. Did I really know the city? Did I like the city? I always said I *wanted* this, but could I really do it? Is this what I still wanted?

My heart was fluttering as the rush of excited energy filled my body, and I was overcome with both absolute joy and complete fear. I was on the work trip with my then-manager and one of my long-time mentors. We spoke about it, but it didn't take long for me to know what I was going to do. I wanted this. Full stop.

Wow, I was really going to do this!

Shortly after I accepted the role, the nerves came back when I realized I'd have to tell my family and friends. I think my family knew this was always a goal, but I don't think they really thought it would happen. Not that they didn't think I could accomplish said goal, but I don't know how serious they thought I was about it.

I distinctly remember telling my sister first—she was happy and supportive, but of course sad I wouldn't be around to watch her firstborn grow through her toddler years firsthand. I strategically planned to tell my mom with my sister by my side, which was not an easy feat considering she had a baby and lived in Washington, DC.

We sat at my mom's dining room table, in what must have been November or December 2016, and shared the news.

❖

My mom cried, but she understood. She wanted me to live my dreams. She was proud and excited but uneasy about the distance. We all were.

Telling my friends was harder than anticipated. They were going to miss me, as I would miss them, and I think we all realized that this meant that things would never be the same again. I kept trying to convince them how much fun it would be when they visited (and visit, they did!).

Once again, I found myself doing what "nice Jewish girls from Long Island" *don't* do. Or don't do alone and unwed, at least. But I was strong in my convictions and desires and wasn't willing to let society put me in a box.

The hardest part, though, was telling my aging and ailing grandmother, whom we were moving back up to New York from Florida just as I would be departing. That hurt. For years, we wanted her to come back to New York after my grandfather passed, but she had a few more good years left in her and, understandably, wanted to live them in her home of twenty-five-plus years.

When I got to Amsterdam, after a few months in, I felt completely lost. This was not because I was in a foreign country and woke up one day wondering what I was doing here. To the contrary, things were going extremely well. I was making friends, I was traveling around the Netherlands and Europe, I was eating amazing food, and I absolutely loved my partial canal view, two-bedroom apartment right off the Prinsengracht canal in the idyllic boutique-lined Negen Straatjes neighborhood (or known in English as the "Nine Streets").

I felt lost because, for almost a decade, the goal had been so singular and focused on *how* to get here. And now that I was there, I didn't know what I wanted next. It was a strange, unknown, and at the time, unwelcomed feeling.

I remember having many conversations with my managers and mentors. Their advice was solid—live in the moment for a little while, and in six months' time, you'll start to write your next development plan and set your next goal.

Six months came and went, and a vague shadow of the next big goal was starting to emerge. It wouldn't be the next role; it might not even be one of the next two roles, but I had a vision and direction again. There was a lot of uncertainty though, in the in-between, about not only how to get there, but how long the journey would take. There still is. The truth is, up until recently, I was sprinting instead of pacing myself for the marathon that is my career, and in doing so, I was missing out on enjoying the journey along the way.

This is something I recently learned to live with and keep in check. It's certainly not easy but having an end-goal and a plan of how to get there keeps me motivated and open as I would journey through this next phase and chapter of my career.

PART 2

THE ADVENTURES OF AMSTERDAYNA

Chapter 14

BECOMING AMSTERDAYNA

It was March 2017 when I officially packed up my Upper East Side studio apartment in NYC and got ready for the adventure of a lifetime. Before my move to Amsterdam, I hosted a going away party at a small dive bar near my apartment. Family, friends, and colleagues from every point of my life stopped by, including several of my UNC friends who came in from North Carolina and Maryland.

The sendoff, which I planned to be low key, ended up being an amazing celebration as I watched friends from all parts of my life mix and mingle. One of my dear childhood friends created an impromptu photo booth setup equipped with props that said things like, "The Adventure Begins" and "Adventure Calls," while another ordered a frozen yogurt cake from one of my favorite shops, 16 Handles. My sister and brother-in-law came up from DC and brought my then 18-month-old niece, Alani. I watched her toddle around as my friends proclaimed how cute she was. It was the best sendoff I could ever have imagined.

During the soiree, my UNC friends started calling me "AmsterDayna." And so then, AmsterDayna was born. Now, there was no turning back. I started a blog to share the adventure with family and friends, and my Instagram handle took on the persona as well.

Six weeks before the big move, I landed in Amsterdam to take care of some administrative work and meet with the new team. Those few days there were hectic—bank and visa appointments, apartment viewings, and onboarding sessions with the team. I was lucky to also sneak in a few dinners with old colleagues and friends. I even did a handoff of a suitcase that I left in Amsterdam with a colleague who kindly offered to store it so I would have some essentials upon arrival.

Pro tip: If you're moving abroad and have the chance to visit before the big move, I highly recommend doing so. What you don't realize when you land is that if you're going straight to your new abode, as was the case with me, you have nothing! After a long journey, all you want to do is take a shower and lie down, but you don't yet have towels, sheets, toiletries, etc., nor do you know where to go to buy them right off the bat—and who wants to spend their first hours in a new country figuring all that out? Yes, you can take it with you in your checked luggage, but that takes up precious room, and you have to factor in that what you may have shipped from home could take several weeks to arrive.

After many tear-filled goodbyes, in March 2017, I zipped up the last of my suitcases, savored my last bites of New York Italian food (pizza and chicken parm!), and used my TSA pre-check to get through security at JFK as a NYC resident for—what I thought could have been—the last time.

I will never forget settling in my seat. I fidgeted nervously with the buckle. I didn't know what to think or feel, as a myriad of thoughts ran through my head: *What will this experience be like? Will I meet friends? Will I like the job? Will my new boss like me? When would I return to the US (as a resident)? Would I ever return? Where does the journey go from here?*

I had about one week to get acquainted with my new home before work began. But my first order of business was finding a sports bar (and new friends) to watch the Tar Heels play in the Final Four match the following Saturday.

I put out a somewhat desperate plea on Facebook the evening I moved to the Netherlands (just moments after the Tar Heels won their

Elite Eight game), asking if anyone knew where and with whom I could make this a reality. To my surprise, an acquaintance from my UNC days came back quickly with what would be the answer to both. He introduced me to my first new friends: a couple from the States, both went to UNC and were now living in Amsterdam. I nervously reached out and was met with a gracious invitation to join them for the games at an international sports café on Leidestraat, or as I like to put it, the Times Square of Amsterdam.

Gonzaga faced South Carolina in the first game, which tipped off at about midnight local time, given the time difference. UNC–Oregon was up next, but when the game rolled around, it would be 3 a.m. My new friends invited me, along with a bunch of others, back to their place to stream the game in the comfort of their canal-side apartment.

Not only were my new friends UNC alums, it turned out one was from Long Island, also a journalism school graduate and worked at the same company as me. Small world! The other worked for Nike, which has its global headquarters based outside of Portland, Oregon, and European HQ outside of Amsterdam. Therefore, I was surrounded by an enthusiastic crowd of UNC fans *and* Oregon fans that evening. I couldn't believe what I had fallen into!

As we sat with our eyes glued to the screen—for me exhibiting both excitement and trying to fight exhaustion—we watched UNC overtake Oregon to advance to the finals! I vividly remember sitting in my Uber cruising down the Herengracht with dawn on the horizon as I watched the streetlights twinkle against the water in the canals. This city was beautiful. No, it was absolutely magical. I couldn't believe this was my new life. It was certainly a successful first Saturday in Amsterdam!

I used Sunday to prepare for my first day of work and to catch up on the sleep I had been cheated out of the night before. I had already made plans to return to my friends' apartment for the championship game, which would be on Monday at 3:00 a.m. central European time.

Monday was also my first day of work. How inconvenient!

As I introduced myself on the first day, I took it upon myself to explain to my new colleagues that I might be a little sleepy on Tuesday, as I had an American college basketball match to watch that evening. I was met with a lot of blank stares. Talk about cultural differences.

Great, another reason to give people a reason to think Americans are ridiculous!

That first evening after work I crawled into bed at 8 p.m. and set my alarm for 2:45 a.m. I had fresh croissants ready to bring over for breakfast. It was definitely a first for all, as none of us ever had a croissant during a basketball game. No one touched them as we sat on the edge of our chairs and watched UNC narrowly eke out the win in a 71–65 victory over Gonzaga.

At 6 a.m., I was back in an Uber for two more hours of shut-eye before I sleepwalked into the office for day two.

Later that same week, I left my apartment in a hurry, as I was running a few minutes behind for a workout session. One important order of business when I moved was finding a gym. Keeping up my physical fitness had become an important part of my routine, and I wasn't willing to make any concessions when I landed in Amsterdam. Luckily, I didn't have to look too far, as there was a gym about 500 feet from my apartment. I connected right away with a local trainer, and it was back to business in a matter of days.

After a good sweat, I rushed home to shower and get ready for work.

I remember thinking to myself on the ninety-second walk back, *Good for you!* I was already waking up early to settle into a fitness routine, enjoying the onboarding at work, making new friends, and absolutely loving my neighborhood and apartment. *I'm doing this, and things are going really well!*

I got to my front door and froze as I realized I forgot to grab my key before I left. I was locked out. It was just nearing 8 a.m., and I had no idea what to do. There I was in sweaty gym clothes, so I couldn't go to work. I also didn't have my laptop. Great. Now I was going to be late. No one had a spare key, as far as I knew. I barely knew anyone here, except for my new UNC friends, who wouldn't be able to help me.

I was pretty sure my trainer wouldn't be able to help me, but I texted him anyway. He came over for moral support and helped look up the name of a locksmith. And then my neighbor bounced down the stairs. He saw me standing outside, clearly locked out, and I told him what had happened.

"Do you have a copy of my key by any chance?" I asked. I was hopeful for a moment.

"No . . . but I have an idea. Wait here!" he said.

He ran inside to get something—the landlord's son lived in the city and had a spare key. My neighbor gave him a call and kindly offered to cycle over to get it. Just like that, I was saved!

I somehow still made it into the office in time, so my completely panicked email to my new boss and predecessor, who was onboarding me, made me look like even more of a whacky person after the basketball comments from earlier in the week. I was so happy though, I didn't care.

It was, for the most part, a time in my life where I had learned to go with the flow and not let the little things trip me up. What were they going to do after all, send me back to the US so soon after my arrival when they had just moved me across the Atlantic? They were kind of stuck with me. It was a freeing and liberating feeling. For the first time in my career, I felt like I had some real perspective.

I was lucky to have a two-week overlap period with my predecessor before she was off on her next gig with the company in Asia. It is so rare that a proper handoff gets to happen. I tried to absorb as much as I could and was grateful for all the introductory meetings she set up. Even though the role was new, I knew that with time I'd figure out the work. I really wanted to focus on getting to know the right people. Who would I need to work with? Who would be able to help me? As I learned years earlier, you need to know people!

Our time together flew by, and then she was off.

I distinctly remember the first time a moment of panic set in. It must've been around my third week. All was going swimmingly until an eyebrow-raising email came in; nothing serious. It contained an ask to help provide counsel on how best to respond to some activity one of our brands was seeing on social media. The person reaching out had no clue I was so new. To her, the ask was completely unassuming and within my remit to take on. I read the tone as "forcefully demanding" as a slight wave of panic came over me. I didn't know immediately how to handle this one or who to turn to in case I couldn't figure it out. As I sat there rereading the email for the third time, my intern asked me a question. I don't remember what it was, but it was something simple. Couldn't she tell I was busy panicking behind my laptop! I wasn't giving her or her question my full attention, but I attempted to open my mouth to respond just as another colleague came up behind to ask something of me. The colleague was asking to begin the handover for something I knew I would ultimately be responsible for moving forward and had been covering it thus far. However, I had no interest in taking it on at that moment, nor did I care to take on this particular piece of work in general. Of course, he picked the worst moment to ask me to take over.

My body temperature was starting to rise as I felt all eyes on me. It seemed like the room was scorching hot, and I needed to figure out fast how to put out the fire. Was I being put to the test by my own team? Did they want to see if I could handle it? To see if I was as capable as my predecessor? Or were they blissfully unaware that I was still new and adjusting and had other things already on my plate?

I remember this moment distinctly because it was the first time in a while I had felt overwhelmed, and it was the first time in Amsterdam that I felt overwhelmed. It was the perfect moment for that pesky thing called anxiety to creep in, but I somehow—for a short moment—willed it away. I took a deep breath and audibly said, "Okay, one thing at a time."

And that's how I tackled each of the other items. One thing at a time.

Years later, I can look back on that moment and be proud of myself for how I handled the situation. I paused, I took a breath, and I pulled the situation back into control by saying I would handle these items task-by-task, one at a time. However, at the time, I couldn't help but feel upset and annoyed with myself. *Why did that happen to me? Was I going to succeed at the job? Was I going to enjoy this job?* The endless stream of thoughts that typically ran through my head started to flow.

It was at this moment that I also remembered the change curve I had been shown during the cultural training I had gone through a few days before. The change curve is a model that helps people understand the different emotional stages they might go through during a period of change or transition. Was I naive in thinking I'd stay in the honeymoon phase forever? Maybe. Where was I now on the curve? How can I get back to honeymoon? Send me back there. I liked it there. Or, better yet, a stable integration.

Thankfully, it didn't take too long to put that incident behind me. After all, there wouldn't be time to stew in it for too long. In such a fast-paced environment, I had to move on. And besides, I was here for a reason. I had worked hard and was about to live my dream. Imposter syndrome be damned!

The Adventures of AmsterDayna had officially begun, and there was a lot more learning—both personally and professionally—on this journey to come!

Chapter 15

HAVING A SENSE OF HUMOR OUTSIDE & INSIDE THE WORKPLACE

I've come to learn in life that having a sense of humor is the bedrock for my own creativity. In my world, I rely heavily on infusions of humor to help tell my stories or make a point (maybe you have noticed by now). That said, I haven't always been like that. I've often been told that I can come across as too serious or uptight. While I fully recognize this, it hurts because I know that is not the real me.

This is why feedback is a gift. If I haven't said it yet, I am saying it here and now. Feedback—real, candid feedback—is a true gift. It's not always fun to hear, and can take a while to sink in, but I've found that after I've been able to sleep on some of the more critical feedback, I end up recognizing what has been delivered. Receiving—and just as importantly, giving—candid feedback sometimes takes a mentality shift. Once you realize that it not only helps you become better, it also helps identify spots you have potentially been unaware of.

But back to humor. There have been moments where my humor has helped lessen tense moments or stressful situations, and there are moments where it has completely backfired and made me want to pull an "Alex Mack" by becoming an oozing puddle of goo that could slink through the walls.

I recently stumbled upon this blog post I wrote to commemorate my six-month mark of living abroad in the Netherlands, and it reminded me just how much of a role humor plays in my life. While this is not a workplace story, I couldn't resist sharing. Therefore, I give you snippets from the blog post entitled:

Six Things I HATE about the Netherlands

I landed in the Netherlands on an unseasonably warm March day. The sun was shining; the tulips were almost in full bloom. The city was bustling. My drive into the city was nothing short of magical. And six months later, that's how it remained: magical.

It was exciting at first to keep track of the milestones: one week in the Netherlands, two weeks, one month, and then two! Early on, I would often hear from people, "One day you're going to lose count," and sure enough, I did.

To celebrate my six-month mark, I did what any normal American (or New Yorker) would do. I tried to think of all the things I hated about my life in the Netherlands. At first, I thought I'd make a list of ten. But I could only get to six. Ironic, I guess. Here are the six things I HATED about living in the Netherlands—one for each month I had been there:

1. The Pizza

I was warned about the Dutch cuisine before moving. I was told it's nothing to write home about. I disagree with that. The native Dutch bitterballen, international eateries, and sheer number of Michelin Star restaurants in a city that's the size of a small village way exceeded my expectations. But my one qualm was the inability to grab a slice of pizza. Sure, there are restaurants that specialize in pizza—real, Italian-style Napolitano pizza. But who wants that? Some days I just wanted a delicious slice of NY-style pizza from Luigi's on the Upper East Side. I missed that. A lot.

2. The Bread

Sticking with the food theme . . . the bread in the Netherlands is so DAMN good. So, why is this on my list of things I hate? I am convinced it contributed to a significant amount of any weight gain. I never used to eat bread so much in the States. I don't know what they do to it, but it is unreal. As is the bread in every European country.

I started each week telling myself that this is the week I will give up bread. For example, one time, I woke up on a Monday and said, "Today's the day." And then I got to work. And had a lunch meeting. And at noon when they broke out the sandwiches, I was hungry. Promise broken. Again. This was actually becoming a serious problem.

And don't even get me started on the butter. If I rarely ate bread in the US, I never ate the butter. It usually came out of a packet and was hard and gross. The butter in the Netherlands is to die for. Fresh, creamy, seasoned to perfection. It's everything you'd want from a pat of butter and more. Delicious!

3. The Hours of Operation

The Dutch are fantastic when it comes to work–life balance. People leave at 5.* Coming from New York, I had never seen anything like it. Truly admirable. But there's nothing special about leaving work at 5 p.m. when everything else around you closes at 5 p.m. Clothing stores, dry cleaning, drugstores. I've never seen anything like that either, particularly coming from a city that is 24/7. I couldn't figure out when you're supposed to pick up prescriptions, buy stamps to mail letters (yes, I still snail-mailed things), and do the millions of other things that come up in life.

Disclaimer: Not everyone leaves work at 5 p.m. and not every day. This also doesn't mean the Dutch aren't hardworking. They are just WAY more efficient at getting things done within working hours, from my observations.

Also, within this bucket, my gym hours. During the week, the gym opens at 7 a.m. and closes at 11 p.m. I was a 6 a.m. gym goer in NY, so 7 a.m. is not that convenient, as it means shorter workouts that allow just enough time to rush home, shower, change, and run to work to be there by 9. It's annoying, but not the end of the world. However, on the weekend, the gym opens at 9 a.m. and closes at 4 p.m.—4 p.m.!—what is that? So, on a Sunday, if I wanted to sleep in and then actually do something during the day, there's zero opportunity to go to the gym at night. That really irks me. Especially after eating so much bread.

4. The Dutch Obsession with Dairy Products

Back to the food. The Dutch are OBSESSED with cheese and milk. Two things I loathe. When I was eleven, one of my friends accidentally spilled milk on me at the breakfast table at summer camp. It sent my disdain for milk through the roof and scarred me for life. I have yet to recover. The

Dutch drink milk with everything and every meal. It totally grosses me out.

As for the cheese thing, well, they certainly love their cheese. Those who know me know I will only eat cheese under the following circumstances: 1. It is mozzarella cheese that is fully baked/melted on pizza or a pasta and accompanied by tomato sauce; and 2. It is orange/yellow cheddar cheese that is pre-grated and completely melted on a macaroni noodle. There is an occasional no. 3, which includes melted [orange/yellow] cheddar on an omelet, but that is absolutely it.

In the Netherlands, there are two kinds of cheese: old and young cheese. I don't know what that means, nor did I particularly care to ever find out. What I do know is that there are a lot of cheese shops, and they smell when you walk by. I lived on a street with an apparently very famous shop. I suppose that's nice for someone who likes cheese. For me, it just became a nuisance, as I had to hold my breath or dodge the cyclists to get to the other side of the road when I walked by.

5. The Weather

The Netherlands is not Spain. No one moves here for the weather. I knew that from day one. I started this post by saying I arrived on an unseasonably warm day, but it never really got warmer than that. For frame of reference, summer in the Netherlands is like autumn in New York. Absolutely beautiful weather to be outside with a light sweater or light jacket. And while it is extremely comfortable to spend a day outside and walk around a city, it's a bit of a letdown for sun worshippers like me. Luckily, there are some incredible beach destinations just a hop, skip, and a jump away.

One of the positives of being so high north is the insane amount of daylight during the summer months. The sun rises at 5:30 a.m. and doesn't fully set until close to 11 p.m. This was an incredible discovery. On the flip side, I don't think I can ever prepare myself for what then comes when winter hits, as the sun doesn't fully rise until 9 a.m. and sets around 4 p.m.

One last note on the weather: the rain. It rains A LOT in the Netherlands. And it's not the put on your raincoat, pop open your umbrella, and you're fine kind of rain. It's the coming at you sideways, no matter what you do, you will get wet kind of rain. I am not a fan.

6. Not Being . . . Dutch

While I fully understand you cannot generalize an entire population, overall,

I noticed there's something about the Dutch that is so admirable. They are direct, which I learned to love. They are practical. They work to live instead of living to work. The latter point is what fascinated me the most. I found that the Dutch have a zest for life. They know how to enjoy every moment of every day, particularly when they are not working.

In six short months, I learned so much from the Dutch. Except for the language. I could not pick up the language.

There you have it. My list of why I HATED the Netherlands.

❈

Just as the outside world might present you with moments when you need to stop and appreciate the humor in a situation, there will be moments inside the work world that will also require you to see the humor in the situation to get by.

During my time in Amsterdam, I was fortunate to work on a lot of projects that had the attention of the global executive team. While working on one such project, a few members of the team had taken over one of the larger conference rooms to work together for the day. It was an intense and ongoing project, but we remained focused and all-in. At some point in the afternoon, having not left that conference room all day, I finally got up to stretch my legs, refill my cup of tea, and go to the bathroom. I was gone for probably all of five minutes, leaving my seat at the table vacant after what must've been at least seven straight hours of occupancy.

In those five minutes, our global CEO decided to pop in and check on the team. Remember, I said it was a large conference room, so there were *several* empty seats (not including my now-vacant seat) free around the table. I came back with a steaming cup of tea in hand and ready to collapse again in my chair only to find it was now taken by said CEO. Oh, and as the only non-Dutch speaker in the room, the conversation had switched from English to Dutch.

All good, I thought. I will just take one of the empty seats. I was more focused on trying not to spill my tea and how I was going to try to pick words out from the conversation given my very, very, very limited knowledge of Dutch. However, as I proceeded to walk in, all eyes turned toward me, and I thought—keyword: "thought"—I saw our CEO start to move. I took the gesture to mean he knew I had been sitting there (obviously! ALL my stuff was there, and the seat must've been warm due to my extended occupancy), and he was now going to get up. So, with a wide friendly smile on my face, I jumped in and said, "Oh no! Don't get up for me. I will sit here," as I nodded at one of the other seats on the other side of the table.

Silence.

Puzzled looks from all in the room.

He wasn't getting up. He had just shifted his weight in what had been *my* chair.

Ouch. Foot, meet mouth.

And to top it off, someone mumbled, "We need to switch back to English."

I like to think I stayed as cool as a cucumber, but I am sure my colleagues will tell you my face went bright red as I squirmed further into my new seat. As I sipped my tea and took in the brilliance of what he had to say to the team on the topic as he reviewed our hard day's work, I couldn't help but glance at my notebook sitting across the table in front of him. Oh, how I wished I had it to jot things down, and oh, how I wished that whole encounter had not just happened!

Did I think this was humorous in the moment? Definitely not. Do I think it is absolutely hilarious now? Of course! The story comes up from time to time with the group of colleagues who were in the room, and I can't help but think about how it provided some comic relief after some very long, intense days.

Chapter 16

LIVING A DREAM

As I settled into my new life in the Netherlands, I quickly made friends. There was an abundance of American expats around my age, which made it quite easy to connect with a plethora of people right off the bat. In many ways, I equated those days to the first year of college—there's so much excitement, and everyone is happy to be there. When you get invited to go somewhere, you say yes. And over the course of the year, you start to realize who you want to keep hanging out with and who you might move on from. All in good spirit, of course.

And work? Work, for the most part, was really great. It was a true challenge adjusting to working in such an international environment, in the best way possible. Most colleagues were older, more established. Colleagues came from all parts of the globe, which I particularly loved. There were very few at the middle-management level like me, and if they were, they were all older than the youngest one in the room—me. I tried not to let that stop me, as I never had before, but admittedly, it did shake my confidence.

It was also the time in my life where I had the highest of highs and the lowest of lows. I was supposed to be here to live my dream.

I always gain energy from my travels and adventures. Work travel took me as close to my new "home" as our cidery in Belgium and as far away as Azerbaijan, Haiti, Argentina, Singapore, and Myanmar. I got to "taste the sun" during the summer solstice in Iceland and visit the forests where a rare yeast, that is the mother to our iconic yeast, was originally found in Patagonia.

Personal travel took me all around Europe—beyond the main cities to stunning jewels like Tallinn in Estonia; Lake Bled in Slovenia; small villages in the Loire Valley, France; and so much more. I was living off the thrill of the next travel adventure and found myself away from home on an average of two weekends each month.

I wrote in my blog as I went, chronicling the experiences I had along the way. I described the terrain, the food, the people, and the culture. Readership was low, but my small audience of friends and family back home was entertained, and I was able to find time to lean into my passion for writing. In fact, it became a highlight of the week to immerse myself in my writing. I reconnected with a creative passion that had not seen the light of day in a long time.

Some of my new friends became family. We spent weekends away together, adventured around our new city together, celebrated holidays—religious and secular—together. We loved on our new home ("How lucky we were to be here," "How wonderful and unique was the shopping," "How the beauty of the city never gets old") and hated on our new home ("Why does everything close so early?!" "Why can I not find this item?" "WHY do they not have NY-style pizza?!"). We cooked and baked at each other's homes together, we explored new restaurants in the city together, and we even tested fad diets (the first time I tried a juice cleanse and participated in the Whole30 cleansing diet!) together. We provided shoulders to cry on in times of need, offered advice on how to get through the tough days, and shared our stash of US medicines when someone was sick.

I was also fortunate to once again be surrounded by an amazing group of colleagues who became fast friends. Our friendships spilled outside of lunches in the office canteen and coffee chats by the bar. Colleagues invited me into their homes and introduced me to their families. We moaned about work, talked about family life, and encouraged each other during the hard days. We came together over wonderful and affordable European wines.

A small group of us came together every few weeks at a different colleague's house for a homecooked meal. Those evenings would last for hours, and the laughter was endless. We were of all different levels, all different ages, and all different cultures. These were moments of such candid joy and happiness.

When Thanksgiving rolled around my first year, I just had to host the group at my place. This was my second Thanksgiving abroad, the first being during my student years in London. While I was a student, I was too inexperienced to cook anything aside from pasta and rice, which did make an appearance as side dishes at this particular Thanksgiving, so the group opted to cater in from an American-style grocery store that catered to the needs of those like us.

However, I was determined to do it the right way this time. I was an adult now, after all, and the responsibility of showcasing an authentic American Thanksgiving meal was resting on my shoulders.

In the days before, I gathered all the ingredients from a combination of local and expat stores. I received my grandmother's stuffing recipe from my mother, as well as my mom's secret tips for making a delicious sweet potato casserole (read: sweet potato with marshmallows). I was prepared for everything except how to actually cook a turkey.

On D-Day, I posted picture of the turkey—raw, naked, cleaned (at least I knew that part), and ready to go into the oven—on Instagram. Moments later I received a message from a good friend who said something along the lines of "You know you need to season it, right?" No, no, I did not. In a moment of panic, I ran out like a maniac to get what I needed. From across the pond, she undoubtedly saved that Thanksgiving!

Seasoning debacle under control, my next feat was to figure out how to manage the oven in my miniature Dutch oven. No, not the Dutch oven that is a pot. I am talking about the ovens commonly found in Dutch homes that are no bigger than a microwave. In fact, they typically double as microwaves. Something I still do not understand.

I worked for hours perfecting the meal, which included many typical sides—stuffing, cranberry sauce, the acclaimed sweet potato with marshmallows, seasonal vegetables, and mac and cheese. I completely overdid it!

When the group arrived, I was overjoyed to share in the delight of Thanksgiving. We started in the living room, easing in with small talk over appetizers and drinks. When we moved into the dining area, I announced my favorite part of the meal. I made everyone go around and share what they were thankful for—an American tradition met with skeptical eyebrow raises by most at the table. After all, cultural differences are real, and to some, sharing deep, personal reflections of gratitude was *so* outside of their comfort zone. Some of the comments were hilariously funny and had everyone roaring with laughter while some were somber—from dating mishaps to beating health scares. After dinner, there was a full dessert buffet, and plenty of wine that flowed throughout the night.

The evening went on for hours, and I never wanted it to end. After all, their departure meant the dreadful task of cleaning up. The turkey grease was everywhere—from the kitchen counters to the floors and my clothes. The red wine tannins were clinging to the bottoms of the glasses, and cake crumbs somehow seemed to multiply. I took it all in and savored the moment. Signs of a wonderful night.

We brought the leftovers into the office the next day for all to enjoy, and I promised to host the full department, not just this small group, the next year.

One year later, this promise was fulfilled. Although the first Thanksgiving will hold a special place in my heart, the second Thanksgiving is one of my most cherished memories to date. Imagine this: about thirty colleagues coming together to share in a meal of thanks. Side dishes and desserts were made by attendees to represent their cultures, as were the beer and wines brought to the table. In this moment, there was no chief of the department who was part of the executive team, and no intern who had just joined for a six-month stint. We were all just people partaking in a meal in a historic canal house apartment on a cold, dark, and wet November night in Amsterdam. It is forever etched in my mind as a true live-in-the-moment memory with everyone sharing what we were grateful for and enjoying each other's company.

When I think back to that special evening, I can still hear the roars of laughter. I see the group squeezed around the table for the main meal. The same table the year prior that was just comfortable enough to seat a third of the attendees now had to fit two-thirds more! Everyone pitched in. A colleague brought folding chairs and a table extender; another colleague cooked a second turkey to ensure there was enough for all.

I can still picture several of us attempting to carve the turkeys without the proper knives to do so. I remember sadly handing everyone their coats and seeing them off as the crowd slowly dissipated as late night turned into early morning hours. My good friend and colleague hung back to help with the cleanup—a welcomed relief this time—as we enjoyed a final glass of wine before finally calling it a night.

The highs of my life abroad weren't all centered around travel, food, colleagues, and friendship, although that of course was a huge part of it. For the first time in a long time, I felt like I was learning and growing. I felt challenged. I had to meander around cultural differences and personalities—every day was a new adventure. Perhaps a minefield to some, I saw it as a playground.

My initial role was to lead corporate reputation and crisis and issues management for our company. These just so happened to be areas of communication where I had little to no experience prior to my first day on the job. That was part of the allure of the job. Not only did it get me back to Europe, it was also a way to expand on my skillset and knowledge. To this day, I am eternally grateful to those who took a chance on me and gave me the opportunity to learn in this role.

There were moments in the beginning when it was daunting, and I found myself letting my boss take the lead instead of proactively jumping in. Normally one to proactively take the reins, or share my opinion, this was so unlike me. I just couldn't seem to find my voice. I kept finding myself sitting in his office as he took the lead and telling myself, *Okay, jump in. Your turn now. You can do this.*

Something was holding me back, and I didn't know what or why this was happening. To this day, I still reflect on these moments and wonder why. The best I've come up with is that some of the issues we faced could have serious repercussions for the business. In that first month or two, I didn't feel confident enough in myself, but really, I was scared to fail, perhaps for the first time. It was an uncomfortable and unfamiliar feeling.

This lack of confidence in my day-to-day had a negative halo effect, even outside of those crisis calls in my boss's office. In our weekly team meetings, I was timid. My voice would crack here and there when I gave an update to the team. I felt like I was a shell of my normal self. And I think people noticed. That was almost the worst part for me because first impressions matter. Typically, I had a strong presence and was not one to give off the meek, one-to-walk-over vibe. Things were not off to a wonderful start.

And then, one day in May, an opportunity to step up came knocking. There was an issue starting to bubble up on social media in some markets in Asia. Then it was in South America. Then the US. And the worst part? It was a resurgence of content from a year or two earlier that came out of an illicit operation in Asia. It was a total fabrication, but to the viewer who did not know this, completely reputation-damaging for the company. As social media does not respect borders, this time, it was spreading faster and wider. I knew we had to act fast to start dispelling the myths depicted in the content while simultaneously working to get it taken down.

One of my colleagues from the marketing team, who sat in another building across the canal but I hadn't yet met in person, came calling, closely followed by colleagues in Asia. It was overwhelming. My boss was out of the office. In fact, most of the senior leaders were away at the annual gathering for the top executives of the company.

A panic came over me. I took a breath and did what I do best. I jumped in.

I pulled together a team. I went back through the old files, which had thankfully been digitally catalogued methodically, to see how similar issues were handled in the past. We got to work, came up with a plan, and worked through the issue the best we could. All of a sudden, I was in my element. Stressed but focused. I was doing this thing! I *could* do this thing.

There was also the reputation management side of the job. I mentioned how science—chemistry in particular—was not kind to me, but math was not my strongest subject area either. Somehow, I scraped by in my education without ever taking a statistics class. This proved to be detrimental to the process while working with one of the top market research firms—in the world—diving into datasets to analyze our company's reputation. My agency partners were patient as I asked lots of questions so I could make sense of it all. This was not something I could just wing. I truly had to learn and understand so that I could then go and explain it to fifty-plus markets worldwide.

Apparently, a glutton for self-punishment, these were the days where taking on too much was no longer the exception. As I was still drawn to building brands, I was able to dabble in providing global PR and communications support to our international beer brands and cider portfolios on the side while doing my "day job." My eyes were always wide open, looking for opportunities. I had yet to realize though, that all of this came with cost: more work meant less time for personal exploration, less time for dating, and less time for friends. It meant dealing with even more senior, opinionated stakeholders. More dotted-line managers to deliver for. It was during these years that I really started to learn the true meaning of "Is the juice worth the squeeze?" and how to truly prioritize.

It was also during these days that I learned to navigate around the complexities of working with senior leaders who gave conflicting feedback.

For example, one day you're being asked to do something because it is perceived to be a strength and your support is warranted; the next time a similar situation rolls around, you find yourself shut out because what was your strength a month ago was now, apparently, perceived to be your weakness. And the hideous cycle continues! What is one to do with this? How do you know where you stand when sometimes you're in and sometimes you're out?

It was during these times that I built greater resilience and my thick corporate skin. I learned to take things with a grain of salt. I also learned to have compassion—you don't know if this person is having a good day or a bad day. You don't know if, in the meeting before yours, someone was told something that shook their confidence or threw them off course. Most importantly, I learned not to take things so personally. All I could do was my best. And if sometimes it wasn't good enough, that was okay. Why? Because I was finally being challenged, stretched. I was *learning*. Professionally, that is exactly what I came to Amsterdam to do.

On a personal note, living and working abroad could sometimes be a sad, lonely place. There were moments when I would walk home from the office at night along the Prinsengracht wondering where life was taking me with all of this. The route home was majestic—the dark night sky magnified the twinkling lights that would glisten along the water. Stunning seventeenth and eighteenth-century canal houses lined the path. The Dutch are a very open culture, to the point where you're invited to "look inside." Window curtains stay drawn through the evening in most homes. You see families sitting down for dinner, couples reuniting after a long day in front of the TV on the couch, and groups of friends gathered together.

I wouldn't have wanted to trade it for any other route home in the world, but the deep questions contemplated on these walks home sometimes did a number on me. *What did I want from a career? What did I want from my personal life? How can I feel so at home here, but so far away from home at the same time?*

My time spent leading crisis and reputation management had been the wildest and most exciting career adventure of my life to date. There were days when I woke up working remotely with the teams in Asia and went to sleep with the team in Brazil. It was completely exhilarating, and I learned a ton.

Although my personal blog and Instagram depicted rainbows and sunshine as I jet-setted across Europe fulfilling my wanderlust, the job was extremely demanding and a recipe for burnout. I also knew it wasn't a forever job, although my desire to remain in Amsterdam may have been forever.

That big question of *What comes next?* continued to weigh on me, and the weight was starting to feel heavier and heavier. If getting to Europe was always the goal, then really, what the heck comes after this?!

Chapter 17

ENCOUNTERING A STALKER

As I embarked on this Amsterdam chapter, I wanted to make sure I was really creating a balanced life for myself. This meant finding time to not only make new friends in my host country but also dabble a bit more in dating.

In February 2017, on my pre-visit trip, I decided to play around with some popular dating apps—just to see who was out there. I was particularly curious to see if JSwipe, a Jewish dating app that has a never-ending list of prospects in NYC, even existed in Amsterdam. It did. And I made it through the list of eligible bachelors in all of thirty seconds.

I connected with this one guy living near the Netherlands, but we didn't start chatting until I was back in the US. The conversation at first was innocent, similar to any other getting-to-know-you conversation. I didn't want to give away too much information for security reasons, but also because I like to save most of the chatter for the actual date. I told this guy that I was going to enjoy my last few weeks in the US spending time with family and friends, and I would reconnect when I moved. Seemed reasonable to me.

Then sh*t got weird.

He started to message me incessantly and eventually found me on Facebook. I did not accept the friend request, but that didn't stop him from sending messages via Facebook Messenger. I was a bit creeped out, but I knew he wasn't based in Amsterdam. He eventually stopped, and knowing I wouldn't reach out to him when I moved, by the time I landed in Amsterdam, the whole fiasco wasn't even on my radar anymore.

Several months later, I was happily settled in my new home, feeling safe and secure. Early September was upon us and the endless daylight season was waning.

One afternoon, I returned from a meeting and the team assistant told me I had a missed call. She rattled off the name of the caller. He had left his number. Hmm. Name sounded familiar, but I couldn't place it. I ignored it and figured if it was important, he would call back.

Fifteen minutes after returning to my desk, a call was put through to me. I picked up the phone.

"Hello?"

"Hi! This is [insert name—I will not disclose]. We connected on JSwipe a few months ago. I am in Amsterdam and would love to see you," a voice on the other line replied.

He called me on a work landline?! He knows where I work? Of course he does. Thank you, LinkedIn.

Sitting in an open-space office and slightly panicked, as well as slightly mortified of what my colleagues would think of any response, I simply hung up the phone. My heart started beating faster.

Five minutes later, the phone rang again.

"Don't hang up. I think you're beautiful and would like to take you to dinner. I can come by your office and pick you up," the voice said.

I had to respond and end this. In a cool, even-keeled tone I responded:

"It is inappropriate to call me at my place of work. Please do not call me again."

Click. I hung up without waiting for a response.

This was probably innocent, but my heart was racing. I had only been in the country for a handful of months. I had no idea how to get in contact with the police—if needed—and if he knew where my office was, could he also find my home address? Was it listed publicly? I had no idea. It is the small details like these that don't matter until they do, and then, as comfortable as your new home has become, you are reminded that you are very much a foreigner in a strange land.

Overhearing the conversation, a few colleagues looked at me with concern. What was that? So I explained somewhat nonchalantly, as I didn't want to cause a scene. Another colleague overheard and suggested we file a police report.

Initially, I thought his advice was a bit extreme, but I was legitimately scared, so I decided to contact a colleague from the company's security team. As luck would have it, I had just been introduced to them a few days prior. I never thought I'd actually have to contact security, let alone for myself!

I went into a conference room and closed the door to place the call. A little shaky, I explained the situation. The security team couldn't have been nicer—did I want someone to accompany me home from the office? They said they could have someone watch my apartment that night too.

We settled on a plan, and they told me to call back if I heard from this gentleman again.

FINALLY, this guy had taken me seriously and stopped calling.

Or so I thought, until there was an email. *He got my email address?!* AND a Facebook message. My blood pressure shot back up again. Now, I was really worried. Who goes to this length for a date when the answer is clearly a no?

I sent the email to the security team, who responded on my behalf and told him to stop contacting me or else they would take action. I never heard from him again after that.

For the next few days, I took extra precautions. I told my neighbors the story and asked them to remain vigilant if anyone should knock on our communal front door. I also took my colleagues up on having a buddy to walk with between our office buildings to different meetings.

Was this guy innocent? I can't say. Was I taking any chances? No!

Did it stop me from dating? No, but it did bring on a bit of a pause, and it continues to put a sour taste in my mouth when it comes to using dating apps. The problem is, in today's world, what else can you do when that is the overwhelmingly popular way to go?

So, what's the lesson here? I suppose it is a reminder that even though we should always be careful about what personal information we put out there, sometimes it is unavoidable. Given the nature of my work, even if I didn't have a LinkedIn account, it is possible to find out where I work and what I do. What I learned from that experience is to remain vigilant, and if something doesn't seem right, do something about it. There are certain things that are just not worth leaving up to chance. Had my colleague not mentioned the police, I cannot help but wonder if I would have gone to the police myself in a foreign country. All I know is if I ever found myself in this position again, I certainly would.

Chapter 18
WORK TRAVEL IS A "PRIVILEGE"

At my first job, a wise colleague taught me an important lesson: work travel is a privilege. At the time, we were getting ready to launch a new cruise ship to the media on behalf of our client. I was focused on securing media to attend the preview launch, and over the weeks of pitching, I came to know the features of this groundbreaking ship inside and out. My conversations with the journalists were going well, and I was quickly filling up spots for the launch.

I became attached to the product, and to the relationships with the reporters, which only ended in disappointment when I found out there would not be a spot for me, the most junior member of the team, at the launch. I understood—really I did—but deep down, it still hurt. My colleague told me that work travel was something that had to be earned; it was a privilege. After all, I had only been working in the real world for three months. What did I expect? (Okay, fine. Insert your entitled millennial-in-the-work-place comment here.)

There's a happy ending to this story. It didn't come in 2010, but in 2011, when we were getting ready to launch the next ship in the series. This time, my hard work was met with what I thought was the ultimate reward: a spot on the next ship to launch! I had no idea, or ever expected, it would be the beginning of a career loaded with work travel.

It was around this time another colleague and friend introduced the word "boondoggle" into my vocabulary. A word that I took much offense to. Why, you may ask? His definition was similar to the dictionary definition, which was explained to be a work trip (or any trip for that matter) that is usually a bit over-the-top, and therefore wasteful, but gives off the allure of having strategic value.

Work travel may be a privilege, and it may take you to some incredible places, but at the end of the day, it is still work. Securing my ticket on the ship didn't mean I was *actually* going on a relaxing cruise vacation; work travel is not a vacation, although my social media depictions of a luxury cruise liner sailing under the Brooklyn Bridge at sunset may suggest otherwise.

Sure, I absolutely love some of the perks that come with work travel: seeing parts of the USA and the world that I may never have had a chance to see, visiting my company's offices in different parts of the globe, and the absolute thrill of reaching a new level of frequent flier status on Delta.

But there are some things I despise: back-to-back travel sprees that last weeks (or even months) at a time, spending less time with family and friends, excessive travel that has broken up relationships and made dating super difficult, interruptions in normal eating and fitness routines, and missing important life events like the wedding of a friend, birthdays, and yes, even the births of all my nieces.

A typical day on the road consists of a 5–5:30 a.m. wake-up call to sneak in a workout before a breakfast meeting. Then it is on to a full day of being "on" in whatever the trip may entail, team dinners or an event, followed by drinks. If you're lucky, you'll get back to the hotel with an hour or so left in the day to catch up on all the work you've missed. All of this when you really just wanted to call it a day around 5 p.m.—shower, order room service, and get into bed before 9 p.m., knowing you have to wake up and do the whole thing all over again the next day.

And then there are those moments where you're standing in a foreign country, or a new US city, and something has gone horribly wrong where you find yourself almost in tears asking yourself, *How did I get here?* These are the best moments to pause and reflect. *How DID I get here? Where did I go wrong here? How can I make this better in the short-term?* and most importantly, *What can I learn from this for the long-term so I never end up* here *again?*

I quickly learned, on that first business trip, that if I was going to take another work trip again (ha!), I'd have to learn how to find a better balance. So that is what I've been striving to do for the last few years: find a better balance. Sometimes it works; sometimes it doesn't. I have yet to perfect it, and it would still take years after this first business trip to learn how to say, "Is my presence really required in person?" a.k.a. "No."

Examples? You want some examples?

Patagonia. 2018. Our colleagues in the US were going to be hosting a press and influencer trip to Patagonia that led attendees on a journey to recount the discovery of the wild yeast that was being used to make a new variant of our product. The US team asked if we wanted to send any global journalists to join the adventure. This wasn't my gig, but my colleague in Amsterdam had a pre-planned family holiday that conflicted with the dates, so he asked if I would manage in his place.

Me? Patagonia? Yes, please!

Remember, at the time, I had the crisis and issues management role, which was an always-on 24/7-type of a job. But with a background in brand PR, this was one opportunity I didn't want to pass on. At least, that is how my mind worked at the time.

Anyway, I worked closely with our agency partner to secure a killer lineup of media and influencers to attend, and off I went on a thirteen-hour and thirty-five-minute flight to Buenos Aires. Upon arrival, we had time to explore the city before flying to Bariloche. Actually, this was "free" time, which would've been used to rest and recharge before an action-packed few days. I saw it as an opportunity to go on an adventure to sightsee while reconnecting with my US colleagues who were on the trip.

When we arrived in Bariloche, my one word to describe it was "breathtaking." The mountains. The scenery. The food. The people.

Our first meal was served lakeside, where our global master brewer did a food and beer pairing while describing how the notes in the beer paired with each course. The next day, we hiked up a mountain, taking in more stunning views. At the top of the mountain, a fiddler—yes, a fiddler—serenaded us on the neighboring mountain peak as we enjoyed our cold beers. The group was enjoying the event immensely—and that's what mattered, right? It couldn't get better than this.

Enter day job. There was an issue going on that had to be managed out of Amsterdam and a social media crisis breaking in Asia. I was glued to my phone, splitting my time between the two. The sun had long set in Europe and had already risen in Asia. And here I was—in the Americas. This was a problem. On top of being severely jet-lagged, I don't think I had properly slept for forty-eight hours. And I am the type of person who needs sleep. It wasn't pretty. My stress level was through the roof, and I was, simply put, profoundly exhausted.

So, what went wrong here? Should I not have gone on the trip? After all, our very capable agency partner was there, as was the team in the US. Did they need me? I like to think yes, but the truth is, probably not. Also, I was covering for a colleague. While he was off enjoying his holiday undisturbed (as it should be), I was trying to pick up the slack for him as well as myself. He had made sure he had a backup. What I didn't do was make sure I had a backup in Amsterdam. Someone who maybe could've jumped in to help me, or at least manage things from a time-zone perspective.

I also should have realized I wasn't cognitively at my best. When it was time for me to go to sleep in the Americas, sleep I so desperately needed, I should've pulled in my boss who was now awake in Europe. I was trying to be all things to all people, and in doing so, perhaps did a bit of reputation damage with colleagues in Asia as I wasn't thinking straight. Was I giving the best counsel and advice? Was I doing anything to help the situation? Or was I slowing us down?

Additionally, I wasn't contributing to making the experience on the ground the best it could be for those whom I was meant to be hosting. They had only a small percentage of my attention. My colleagues had to pick up my slack, which was possible as there were several colleagues from different markets and support from our PR agency. This again brought me to the question of *Did they even* need *me or someone from my team here?*

I remember returning back to Amsterdam exhausted and with my head held a bit low. While we still received incredible output from the journalists, I couldn't help but wonder if the output could have been even better or stronger had I been 100 percent present. It was also one of the first times the trip went beyond just working with traditional media (journalists). As there were multiple parties on the trip—media, influencers, US restauranteurs—could we have divided and conquered on our end to provide more personalized experiences to each audience instead of pooling resources and trying to force one itinerary to fit all? These were still the early days of working with influencers, and we were slowly learning that traditional journalists and influencers merit different approaches. Had I been fully present and recognized this on-site, could we have tackled this in real-time and adjusted accordingly?

The post-mortem discussion on this trip was a deep one. We all learned a lot—those who were on-site and those who stayed behind in Amsterdam.

My Instagram, though? Great content! Photos on top of stunning mountains, cute shots of cheers with beers, incredible up-close footage of where the wild yeast strain came from in its native environment. Instagram versus reality at its finest.

But wait, there's more.

Azerbaijan. 2019. UEFA Europa League finals. I had moved on from the crisis and issues management role and was back to brand PR, supporting our international beer brands and cider portfolios out of Amsterdam.

One of our brands was a sponsor of the UEFA Europa event. I

saw this as an opportunity for media and influencers to learn about our historic brand, its sponsorship strategy, and get a front row seat to some incredible soccer (errr, football). This would be a first for the brand, and my marketing colleagues were very supportive of the idea.

I landed in Azerbaijan the night before the action started and will never forget walking through the pristine airport. At customs, I was given a keychain and a rose. Well, that was lovely. Welcome to Azerbaijan!

As the company had arranged for many stakeholders to come in for the event from multiple countries, I met the group I'd be traveling to the hotel with at the airport—and we were off. During the ride to the hotel, I used the time to check emails and catch up on what I had missed while in flight.

The next day, I met the group of press and influencers we gathered, and the program got underway. We started with a press briefing from the head of the brand before setting out to enjoy a special activity that we had planned before the big game. It was a great group, and all was going well.

And then my phone service shut off.

I received a series of text messages in Dutch from the mobile provider, which I could not read. We finished out the afternoon and headed back to the hotel, where I would be able to connect to Wi-Fi and figure out what was going on.

Once back in the hotel, we had only thirty minutes to change and head back out to the game. My heart was racing as I tried to simultaneously get ready and fix the phone issue.

A Google translation told me I had gone over my allotted minutes for roaming and my phone service had been suspended. If I wanted to reinstate service for an extra charge, I needed to respond with "Ja" ("Yes" in Dutch). "Ja," "Ja," "Ja" . . . didn't work.

I emailed some folks in Amsterdam with an SOS to see if they could help. Silence. It was a Saturday.

So, here I was in Azerbaijan and in charge of eight people, all relying on me as the point of contact in this very foreign land. And once we left the haven of hotel Wi-Fi, there was no way to be in touch. How did people live before smartphones?

It took a good twenty-four hours for assistance to come and for my phone to be up and running, just in time for our flights home. Fantastic.

I learned a very important lesson here: never assume that your company phone plan is unlimited, especially if you are American and living outside the US. Chances are it is not. And your phone service will shut off on you at the most inconvenient time and most unfamiliar of places. This could've been avoided if I had the foresight to check and make sure I was good to go, and to see if my phone plan had any limitations.

There was another moment on this trip when my heart sank deeper into the pit of my stomach. On the day after the game, there was some time to explore our surroundings, and I offered our guests a few options. The group voted overwhelmingly for a half-day exploration trip to the mud volcanoes of Azerbaijan. So, to the mud volcanoes we went!

Our driver picked us up in a legitimate-looking tourist minibus with the company branding on the side. So far, so good. He offered commentary about the sites out the window along the way. He wasn't the most engaging character, but I think everyone was enjoying some quiet time after the excitement of the premier football game the day before. At one point, we pulled up to a group of locals stationed off the side of the road, standing alongside their 1950s Soviet-looking automobiles that had seen better days. Our now seemingly luxurious minibus came to a halt and the driver turned around to say: "Okay, out you go. These gentleman will take you on the next leg, as my vehicle is too large for the roads."

Uhhh, what?! Heart, meet pit of stomach.

I asked the guide if he would be coming with us, and he said no. He would be waiting for us upon our return. This wasn't a good enough response for me. I insisted he vacate his vehicle and join us, and expressed my disappointment that this was not explained to me when we reviewed the itinerary days prior. Nor was it mentioned in the plethora of reviews I had read about the experience. I think he could see the look of panic in my face and—realizing I was a petite female about to go off-roading with a group of all-male journalists *and* a group of strange local men—took pity on me. He came along.

As we split up into groups of two to three and piled into the cars, I asked my fellow carmate to track us on Google Maps (remember, I had no phone). I think the only thing that gave me even the slightest peace of mind was seeing that another mini tour bus had pulled up behind us. Their (mixed-gender) group was about to embark on the same journey. That said, I don't think I was able to breathe for the fifteen-minute drive, unsure of where we were going. Talk about being outside your comfort zone.

After what seemed like an eternity, we arrived at this complete ecological wonder. You looked left—barren land. You looked right—barren land. Nothing but a gray horizon in all directions. And then these piles of mud came into view. It looked like a middle school science fair project where clay was forced into the shape of a volcano. As we leaned in closer to the center of the pile, we could see the mud boiling. And the smell? It was as if you were surrounded by rotten eggs. Then, every so often the volcanoes would erupt, and a gush of mud lava would flow down the sides of the tiny one-to-three-foot volcano, adding to the messy layer of sediment already coating their exterior.

We were all deeply entranced by the cyclical nature of it all. It was bizarre, unlike anything I had ever seen before. It was messy and gross, beautiful and mysterious. I still wasn't convinced we weren't about to be sold off to a terrorist organization, even though signs of that happening were lessening.

With my heart still in the pit of my stomach, we got back into our shouldn't-be-in-use Soviet relics and made our way back to the tour van. Seeing it in full view was a blissful site. The bus ride back was energetic. The media thoroughly enjoyed the experience and couldn't stop talking about it. Although I breathed a heavy sigh of relief, I was still shaken up inside.

I never slept better on a redeye than I did on this flight back to

Amsterdam that evening. Never again would I go somewhere with a nonoperational phone. Never again would I plan an adventure in an unfamiliar and foreign land on my own without the support of a professional agency.

My Instagram, though? Incredible content! I had fantastic photos from the "big game"—watching Chelsea (the underdog and my pick!) beat Arsenal. I happily documented our media and influencers creating tifos—artwork made by soccer fans to cheer on their team—with a local artist to bring to the game. And of course, there were photos of the history-rich walking tour through Old Town Baku, and the ecological wonder that is the famed mud volcanoes of Azerbaijan. Instagram versus reality strikes again.

Before I learned these lessons the hard way, I didn't do myself any favors. I fell deep into the trap of oversharing and inadvertently glamorizing my life over social media. After all, how many times have you found yourself looking at someone's Facebook or Instagram feed and thought *That person's life is amazing,* or *They are the luckiest person in the world!* Social media envy is real, and no one is immune to it.

I am typically met with, "You're so lucky," and "I wish I had your job." I wouldn't disagree. I think I have one of the best jobs in the world, but it's not for any of the reasons you would pick up from social media.

That said, herein lies another hard lesson in the age of social media. I am the firmest believer that while work travel can be a privilege, it is hard. Very, very hard. And exhausting. By glorifying it, I was giving off the impression it is fun and games all the time. That it was a walk in the park that didn't impact my own well-being or cause unhealthy levels of anxiety at various times. But that is just not true. I was lying to myself and to others.

I am now very careful with what I choose to share on social media, both from a work and personal perspective. I'm not interested in misleading or—in some cases—creating a window into a world that doesn't exist. And my wish is that others will stop and think about that too.

Chapter 19

BOUNDARIES AND BORDERS

When I arrived in Amsterdam, I thought I was going to stay forever. In fact, early on I even started looking at real estate, lured by the fact the Dutch do not put down payments on properties (or are not required to) as compared to a 20–25 percent down-payment requirement for an apartment in NYC.

To this day, almost two years later, I still cannot believe I am no longer there.

When my initial two-year assignment as the crisis and reputation management lead was over, I had the option of continuing on in said role or moving to a different position on the team. While the work was challenging and fulfilling, and it allowed me to work with colleagues from around the world, I realized it was taking a toll. I work well in fast-paced environments, but when every day involves a new fire drill, at some point, it gets old. I was starting to feel burnt out.

There was an opportunity to move back to the brand PR side. The role I had temporarily occupied when I first arrived in Amsterdam as a side gig, before it became someone else's full-time job, was available again. I saw this as an opportunity to jump back in and really shape something that hadn't yet truly come to fruition. So I jumped.

I always saw this as an interim position until I figured out what was next within the organization. I thought there would be a new and exciting role in a different market or within one of our regions. Even though there was some good opportunity in this new role, it wasn't enough of a challenge to satisfy me long-term. The urge to move on had come knocking, but I was starting to view Amsterdam as home. The hope was that some other challenge would come up and keep me in Amsterdam. I was desperate to have a direct report or manage a team. My experience prior to the Amsterdam move was way too short, and I just knew it was something I was meant to be doing.

There was one problem. I never communicated my plan to anyone. I assumed my boss knew that this new role was meant to be a placeholder because it didn't provide the challenge and growth opportunity I so desperately needed to stay content. This plan only lived in my head because I was somewhat ashamed of not being able to name what *exactly* I wanted next. It seems strange for someone like me, especially since I had been an open book in my younger years, making my ambitions known and working with my managers to help get me there.

I suppose you could say I was still floating, unsure of what *was* next. This job allowed me to strategize and sit at a big kids' table—the management team table of the international brands team to be exact—but it was just as tactical as it was strategic. I was a team of one with limited resources who was trying to showcase how brand PR could provide a positive business impact from a global perspective.

I loved being in the historic heart of our company's headquarters, but I was starting to realize I needed to get out of my own way. I was holding myself back by retreating in many ways instead of progressing, and every time I took a step forward, it seemed like it was then followed by two steps back. For example, here I was going back to my brand PR roots instead of continuing to expand upon and grow my overall corporate affairs capabilities. This wasn't a bad thing; it just wasn't right for me. Even though I was good at this type of job and comfortable, I started to realize it no longer meant that it would make me happy. It wasn't challenging enough. I was so caught up on the hamster wheel that I couldn't see beyond the immediate. I started to recognize it as behavior associated with the early days of my first job all those years ago.

Personally, I continued on the path of travel domination—physically crossing borders at every chance I could get, while professionally, I was losing my boundaries.

I was unable to say no, taking on projects that were under-resourced. I was losing respect for myself, even though, ironically, I was gaining respect from some of the more senior commercial members of the company.

It was a paradoxical mix of emotions, to say the least. One thing was becoming abundantly clear: for the first time in my career, I felt this strange sensation that I was losing my voice. I wasn't succeeding in advocating for myself—for what I wanted and needed to be successful and happy.

Throughout my career, I had fallen victim to doing things I knew were the right thing to do for the company or brand, yet I had not been properly set up to do them successfully. My positions had been under-resourced in terms of having reasonable support to complete a project, but I still managed to overdeliver on the results.

This was a complete, double-edged sword. Unable to accept failure or defeat, I'd fall into the same trap of delivering the impossible and making it look easy. But it wasn't easy. Anything but. Behind my own curtain, I was a workaholic who put work before friends, work before family, and work before health. Sleep was forgone, and weekends given up, since there just weren't enough hours in the workweek to get it all done. All the while, running myself ragged over the years. I'm not sure how many times I fell into this trap. It was a trait that started way before my days as AmsterDayna but seemed to get worse during my time in Europe because I was inadvertently letting it.

In one instance, I took a week off while my mom was visiting, and we spent it together in the Czech Republic. I successfully convinced her to climb around 300 steep steps in the August heat to get to the top of Prague Castle Tower. It must have been about 100 degrees Fahrenheit (around thirty-seven degrees Celsius)! As she begrudgingly trailed slightly behind me, her face shifted from miserable to furious as I took a call from someone in the office—an attempt to solve some trivial issue that had come up. In another, I was celebrating my thirtieth birthday over a long weekend in the incredible town of San Sebastian, Spain, with four friends. It was Friday, and my actual birthday. It was a day we had all taken off from work to celebrate *me*—and here I was, sitting in the hotel room answering emails from my boss's boss, while my friends patiently waited on me so we could go take in the scenery.

In June 2019, after one such experience, I finally decided I would no longer be a victim of this type of circumstance.

I was in Iceland. One of our brands was sponsoring a music festival during the summer solstice. Twenty-four hours of daylight! As part of this current role, it was my job to figure out how to raise global awareness for the brands that were not well known in most geographies outside the brand's home country.

The strategy here was to introduce journalists who had global audiences to this specific brand and what it stood for. In this case, the brand's positioning was connected to and revolved around the sun. The sponsorship of the festival was key for the marketing team to bring the brand to life in an experiential way, and since everything was already planned by my marketing colleagues, I saw this as a low-hanging fruit opportunity to bring journalists along on an already existing program.

One problem: as this part of the program was a last-minute add-on, there were very limited—read: no resources—to support it. The approved budget only covered the cost of bringing the three journalists on the trip, and no more. This meant that I wouldn't be able to engage one of our agency partners—who normally handled everything from securing media attendants to taking care of any logistic issues on the ground throughout the duration of the trip—to support me and the program. This would all be on me.

Now I can almost see you sarcastically rolling your eyes and saying, "Oh, poor Dayna," as you read this. "She has to do it on her own. Isn't this her job?"

Well, no, not really.

At the time, I was supporting upward of ten different brands. It is impossible to lead strategy and execution on ten brands, which is why most corporates rely on the brilliant support of agency partners. Recall in the earlier chapter where I talked about my role on the agency side in supporting the launch of the cruise ship. I was doing this type of execution work on behalf of my client. And remember, it took place in my first years out of college.

But all these years later, I was unable to say no to what was better for the company's interests than my own because I was so determined to show that brand PR could make a positive impact on a global level. The hope was that next time, incorporating PR into the overall marketing plan wouldn't be an after-thought and I would have the proper timing and resources from the start. I was sacrificing myself and my sanity to orchestrate a better future. Once again, I was unable to admit that success wouldn't be possible without the proper resources. I was still thinking I could keep making the impossible possible.

So, off I went, securing the media, booking their travel, communicating their itineraries, managing their expectations, etc. Admittedly, I was able to obtain some of the team intern's time to support me, but at the end of the day, she wouldn't be the one conversing with media in the off-hours, and I was on my own for the duration of the trip, which was taking place over the weekend.

I landed in Iceland on a Friday, and the first of three reporters arrived. We connected just before the program was scheduled to begin. However, the other two reporters were experiencing massive travel delays and, as it was already the weekend, any support at the home office in Amsterdam was over.

The reporter and I had no choice but to get on the bus and go, and with no backup on the ground, I needed to figure out how I was going to meet the others once they landed in Reykjavík. We joined a larger group for dinner that first evening, and as I chatted with Reporter No. 1, I found myself constantly apologizing while on my phone playing travel agent for the other two. Thankfully, she was incredibly sweet and understanding—otherwise, this could've been even more of a disaster.

Reporter No. 2 was only slightly delayed. He would arrive midday Saturday, which meant he'd have to miss the first activity of the day. A bummer, since it would be a deejayed event in a glacier. Wait, what? Yes, you did read that right. However, he'd make it for the afternoon festivities and beyond.

Reporter No. 3, the US-based reporter, was a different story. Her flight itinerary included a layover in NYC, but her originating flight was delayed, so her evening flight from JFK Airport to Iceland departed without her.

I counted down the minutes until that Friday night dinner was over so I could flip open my laptop and resume my role as travel agent, this time for Reporter No. 3. I secured a hotel room for her overnight stay in NYC, arranged Uber rides between the airport and the hotel via my phone so she wouldn't have to foot the expense, and successfully booked a Saturday flight to Reykjavík.

Friday night was meant to be the night to "get sleep" because Saturday was going to be an all-day affair. After all, you come to Iceland for the summer solstice and get to witness the sun at its best for twenty-four hours straight.

Given the time difference between the US and Iceland, I was up for hours trying to sort all the arrangements out for our last guest. Even our company travel agency was unreachable and, quite honestly, not helpful at all when they were in touch. Thanks for nothing.

Once Reporter No. 3 had been taken care of, I turned to finish some other work (remember, I was responsible for nine other brands that didn't care that I was away with this one!). When my head finally hit the pillow. It was about 2:30 a.m., and my alarm was set for 7 a.m.

In bed, I waited for sleep to come but it was nowhere to be found. I was furious. Beyond furious. The tears started streaming down my face. I was overtired, that was for sure. Naturally, at first, I was mad at everyone else. And then I got real. I was mad at myself. I started wallowing down a path of self-pity. Instead of trying to find the positives and fill my head with things I loved about my job, I was making a list of everything I hated. I counted everything I resented about work that night instead of counting sheep. This was not helpful. Not helpful at all.

The next morning, I was a zombie. It was Saturday, so luckily the volume of other work was dialed down. However, I knew I wouldn't be fully present until each of the three journalists in my care had two feet on the ground—in the land of fire and ice—and were under my watchful eye. This brought about unwelcome feelings of anxiety. *Do glaciers typically have good cell phone signals? Would I be able to keep in touch with the absentee journalists who were still en route to us?*

As the hours ticked on, Reporter No. 2 found us. One sigh of relief. And Reporter No. 3 joined us much later in the day. Double sigh. Both made it in time for our next big event: a live concert in a 4,000-year-old lava tunnel. Yup, you read that one correctly too.

Upon my return to Amsterdam, I went straight into a full week of meetings. I remember my boss asking me, with wide eyes, how it went. I decided to be straight up with him (and myself). Yes, it was an incredible itinerary, but it was a nightmare of a trip. I told him I hoped we'd never put anyone in that situation again, and I, for sure, would not be doing something like that ever again.

That moment of reflection was profound. I learned a mind-altering and life-changing lesson here—no matter how great the opportunity—nothing, absolutely nothing, was worth doing without the proper funding and resourcing. Was it worth it in the end? No. Actually, it was not. Not only had the whole experience sent me down a dark "I strongly dislike my job" spiral, but as an output, we only received one piece of coverage from the three reporters who attended. I was mortified that the project had failed. This had never happened to me, and after the insanity of the experience, that hurt. It hurt a lot.

A colleague and good friend once told me something that stuck. She said, "Your team never drops the ball." She then went on to say, "Sometimes you need to let the ball drop for you—and most importantly others—to finally realize how under-resourced you are."

So, at the end of the day, was that press trip *really* worth it? For me personally, I suppose then the answer was yes. I say yes here because I finally learned that I needed to change a negative and self-damaging behavior that had been taunting me for years: once and for all, I had to stop taking on projects that were not deemed important enough to warrant the proper resourcing necessary to help make it a success.

I also learned to be candid with the feedback I gave my superiors. I learned to stop sugarcoating things. When something goes wrong and provides an opportunity for learning, it is more important than talking about the glacier or lava tunnel or helicopter ride over the Eurasian and North American tectonic plates!

Chapter 20

ALL GOOD THINGS . . .

No one forced me to leave Amsterdam, although I may have acted like it wasn't my idea at the time. It was my decision and my choice. One that confused many people—myself included. On the outside, I was living my dream. I was in Europe. I was gallivanting everywhere and loved my life here. I made friends who had become family. I never let on at work that I was unhappy with my role. No one was aware of the lessons I was learning. To be fair, most of the time, neither was I. I never complained. I just kept going and did it all with a smile.

It may have seemed like a rash decision to move back to the US, but with most things in my life, it was not.

The environment around me was changing fast. Working in a global head office can be transient, as a lot of the workforce moves between the global HQ and local markets every few years. Multiple changes were coming to all the senior stakeholders I worked directly with, as they were heading off to their next assignments, moving within or outside the company.

Change doesn't scare me. But there was one question at hand after a few years of intense work in a matrix organization, where you spend significant time networking and influencing in order to get something done. The question was: *Did I really want to go through that again with all new colleagues?* and maybe more importantly, *Do I really want to do that in a role I am already frustrated with and I know is not long-term? Was it worth it? Did I have the energy for it?*

I had to take a hard look at my life. Was my lifestyle healthy? How much longer could I keep up this game of running around to a different city or country every other week? I was too tempted by the ease of travel around the continent. Travel was my source of inspiration—it always has been—but it was also becoming a source of exhaustion.

And what about prioritizing my personal life? I left little time to date or to think about what I really wanted from a long-term relationship. *Do I want to ever get married? Do I want kids?* I never felt a strong desire for either as some of my friends did, but I was never opposed to it happening. *How will I ever know what I want if I don't try?*

I had a few options:

1. Wait it out and see what happens, or what other opportunities open up within my company network worldwide.

2. Call around to the team in the US and see what's possible there.

3. Leave the organization.

Learning from years past, when deciding how to start my career, I knew staying in my head, and my head alone, would be damaging. Big decisions, particularly life-altering decisions, are dangerous to make in isolation. While at the end of the day the decision should be yours, having an external sounding board to provide perspective helps you see the clear light. At the very least, I learned you need to write it down—either with pen and paper—or type it out. Whatever your preference, just get it out of your head.

I knew I needed to call in several resources to help me collect my thoughts on this one, so I immediately started making phone calls. I spoke to family members, mentors, and trusted Amsterdam colleagues. And I called my former Amsterdam colleague and friend who I greatly respected and happened to be leading the corporate affairs team in the US.

As if it were fate, one of the only roles I would've considered on the team in the US had just opened up. It wasn't my dream job, but it was a really good job. It kept me with the company and got me back to the US to reevaluate my life, as I started to chart the next chapter and course of both my life and career. It also came with a direct report, which was extremely important to me for the next step in my career.

Within a matter of hours, I knew that options one and two were both good ones. Now came the tough part: I had to decide what was the best course for me—one, two, *or* three.

A day or so later, I found myself in a W Hotel room in Warsaw, Poland—traveling over the weekend again for a work-related event— writing out a messy pros and cons list on the miniature pad of paper by the phone that's probably not meant to outline your life's plan.

It was early spring, but could've been the dead of winter as I stared out into an overly gray sky. There was a chill in the air, and I remember feeling so uncertain and dreadfully alone. I was also cold. Really cold.

I took my scratches of paper back to Amsterdam and showed them to a few trusted friends. It was 2010 all over again. Everyone had a different opinion, and this time they were all over the map. Literally!

Some questioned if leaving the place I had grown to love and wasn't ready to leave was really a smart move. Some thought that after six years with my current employer, it was likely time for a change. Some wondered if it was wise to consider working for a close friend. Some saw a move back to the States as a potential for a much-needed reset. And others weren't surprised I wanted to make a move; they just didn't think I would even consider a move back to our business in the US.

This time, I graciously took what everyone had to offer and then cleared my head. The decision did not belong to them. It was mine. I knew what I was going to do.

PART 3

COMING [BACK] TO AMERICA

Chapter 21

THE START OF THE REPATRIATION GAME

M y final day with the global team in Amsterdam was July 4, 2019. A symbolic day for many reasons. Colleagues from around the business joined me for farewell drinks—a somewhat paradoxical tradition of sending off those we care about as we mourn the fact that our dear colleague is moving on from us while merrily celebrating what's next for them. The farewell celebration was then followed by a Fourth of July party at my boss's house, complete with a BBQ and sparklers. It was truly a wonderful sendoff given by a group that had become more like family and friends than colleagues.

When I made my decision, one thing was clear: I needed to reset. I needed a real reset. And that meant I needed a break. I thought that after a decade of running full-speed at 200 percent and giving my all to my career, two months off sounded reasonable. I understood now why "gap years" are so popular—outside of the United States—and why taking a sabbatical is not frowned upon.

It wasn't an easy sell, but thankfully I had the support of both my direct manager in the Netherlands as well as my new boss in the US. In retrospect, two months wasn't nearly enough, but we'll get to that in a bit. At the time, it was a huge win.

And there was another key lesson learned—never stop fighting for what you believe in. I was not going to back down in my quest to take that time off. I recognized that I needed it in order to be the best version of myself for this new role. In hindsight, that is something I am proud of, rather than ashamed. It is one of the first times, after so many years of being told to do so, that I put myself first.

I used those two months to leisurely pack up my place in Amsterdam, check a few things off my Dutch bucket list, read some good books, and get in a few more travels with friends. I soaked up all the European sun I could before that dreaded date of August 27, 2019, when a KLM flight would take me away.

A one-way ticket to New York–JFK. As I settled into my seat, I didn't cry as I thought I might. I held my head high. I was proud of what I had done. Three years earlier, I got on a plane and headed to an unknown place. I showed up as a twenty-something and I owned it. I made friends. I traveled the continent. I worked hard and made an impact. I came here to live—and live, I did.

As I selected my first movie from the in-flight entertainment screen, a commercial for one of my company's products came on the screen. I smiled. I knew the colleagues who had made this commercial. I had been part of the conversation, part of the process, for this particular ad. Seeing our advertising was not new for me; it's everywhere! But yes, in that moment, I was proud. I was damn proud.

Once we were wheels-up, there's only one word to describe that seven-and-a-half-hour journey: melancholy. I stared straight ahead. Unlike when I left for Amsterdam, there was no cheerful handwritten plane letter from my mom to be read, gearing me up for my next big adventure, and no foreign country on the other end to receive me. However, there would be reunions with family and friends who were overjoyed to have me back, a new apartment in NYC to find and settle into, and the endless opportunity to eat all the New York-style pizza my heart desired. There was no question I would make the best of this new chapter, no matter what it threw my way.

❖

When I got back to the US, one month and three weeks of travel were behind me, and I had only one week left before starting work again. BIG mistake.

In an effort to stay in Europe for as long as possible, I significantly underestimated what it would take to reacclimate after returning to the US.

My friends all wanted to see me, I needed to find a place to live, *and* I was about to start a new job.

It was going to take six-to-eight weeks for my container to arrive from the Netherlands, so I was living out of the suitcases I brought with me on the plane.

All the weight I had accumulated over the course of my summer of eating was starting to show, and my clothes felt tight.

Oh yeah, and even though I *thought* I wanted to come back to New York, I was already starting to question if I even *belonged* in New York anymore. It was my home city and a place I'd always love, but I had changed so much—maybe it was no longer for me?

Things that never bothered me about it started to become more noticeable—I started finding it to be dirty, smelly, hot, and crowded. I couldn't see the beauty I once saw, and instead found myself comparing it to the charming cobblestone streets and simplicity of life in Europe. The energy of the city that never sleeps that used to propel me forward in my day-to-day was now unwelcomed and overwhelming.

To combat that, I was trying to stay up-to-date with friends and colleagues in the life I just left while also trying to rejoin the life I was about to rebuild. That didn't work. It didn't enable me to fully let go, which kept me from being fully present.

Within my first week, I got off to a rocky start with some colleagues at work. This had never happened to me before. Admittedly, being fresh off the boat from Amsterdam, I had a newfound ego that wasn't doing anyone any good—especially me. I found fault with everything and everyone. I was rejoining a completely changed organization from when I had left it. I knew this would be the case, but experiencing it firsthand was hard. This transition was painful, unlike my experience in Amsterdam, where a culture expert coached me on all things "Netherlands" for two days, which contributed significantly to my smooth landing.

And here I was, back on my home turf, with no help or support. No warning that coming back would be way harder than going.

In my quest to make a move, I realized that I hadn't asked all the right questions about my new role. Of the questions I did ask, I don't know if I really listened intently to the answers. Of the answers I heard—and wrote down—some just didn't prove to be accurate upon arrival. Some things had also changed within the team and organization as a whole between the time I accepted the job offer in April 2019 and when I started in September. I had made some assumptions and thought certain things would just fall into place as they always had before.

I felt smothered, overwhelmed, and so unsettled. I felt like a failure and a disappointment at work. I also felt like an unavailable friend, daughter, sister, and aunt. Simply put, I was miserable.

Things were off to a bumpy start!

To make matters worse, I started to realize just how burnt out I was, and how I had not used my two months wisely to rest and recharge.

My mind traveled back in time. Just under a year into my career, I remember getting some wise advice that I had tuned out at the time. I had been working hard and it was being recognized. In a rare moment that found me alone with the most senior member of the team after a client call, she took the opportunity to tell me I was doing a great job. She even joked that half the office would be working for me one day. I laughed. It was flattering but ridiculous. In those days, I never imagined that could be possible.

But she also had some advice. Advice I took lightly at the time. She told me I was going to burn out if I kept going at my current pace.

At the time, I thought, *Me? Yeah, right. She doesn't know me.*

So I kept running.

Toward the end of the Forrest Gump movie, he puts on a pair of trainers, and he runs for three years. It's ridiculous. Everyone who watches the movie thinks so.

But in 2010, I put on a pair of heels and, metaphorically, started to run. By the end of 2019, I had been running full-steam for almost ten years.

At least Forrest wore sneakers. I was mostly in heels. And people called him stupid?

In all seriousness, though, I was beginning to realize how real burnout was.

I remember vividly arriving in the Netherlands and hearing of colleagues who were on "burnout" leave.

"What's that?" I asked my boss.

He proceeded to explain that it was essentially a leave of absence granted to those who had been deemed too burnt out to work by a psychologist or physician. I couldn't believe it!

All of New York City was in some stage of burnout, yet in the US, there was no such thing. I was envious, once again, of the Dutch. This time, for their belief in and acceptance of a serious human condition.

Chapter 22

A NOTE ON RESILIENCE

I am nothing if not resilient. Sometimes I can recognize it, and sometimes I momentarily lose sight of it. I am human, after all.

I believe my resilience stems from my childhood.

To the outward world, I grew up privileged. I lived in an upper middle class suburban town on Long Island, New York, and had my own bedroom and a backyard. The high school I attended is consistently rated as top ten on Long Island and top 500 in the United States. But as the saying goes, you never know what goes on behind closed doors.

As I recalled earlier on, I grew up with a verbally abusive father who would rather see his wife and children live on the street than leave us alone in peace in his own self-described castle. He was the king, after all. The great one. As we were told almost daily.

It wasn't always this way, at least not to my recollection. I began to notice things were off around the age of ten when I was in fourth grade. I was a perceptive child. I picked up on things other kids my age didn't. Maybe because my eyes were always wide open. They had to be.

When I was around eleven, I was upstairs with my sister on a Saturday night, and my parents had just returned home from a night out with their friends. I heard arguing downstairs.

I tiptoed down the stairs in an oversized f.r.i.e.n.d.s t-shirt, pajama pants, and my untamed, pre-teen red hair. These were the days before I was introduced to styling gel and the magic of straightening irons. The stairs led to the pathway into the kitchen where I saw my father clutching a knife—my mother's face pale. They both looked at me. All three of us, terrorized. The knife was put away. No one was hurt physically. My mom went to her bedroom, and I went back upstairs. My father retreated to his office in the basement. We never spoke of the incident.

My father didn't leave his castle—by force—until I was fifteen. You could say, by then, that the damage had been done. But I would never look at myself as damaged. Far from it. As I shared earlier, I was always an observant child and these years built my hypervigilance. Although I may have always been on edge, those were the years I also built my resilience. Those years made me a survivor. And I wasn't alone. I had my mother and my sister. And we all had my maternal grandparents.

I adapted the "sticks and stones may break my bones, but words will never hurt me" saying to fit my situation—and to get through the day. But I now realize the adage is wrong. Words are the foundation of bullying. Words can kill. If only the second half of it read, " . . . but it is the resilience I build that will ensure no one can ever hurt me."

I share this now as important context to my story. It was decades later that I was finally able to describe where my resilience came from.

I never wanted to be a statistic of a broken family. Therefore, as I shared earlier, everything I did, I did to show the world that kids like us can succeed.

Everyone builds their resilience in different ways. The process and the individual journey should not be seen as more challenging than the experiences of the friends who stand by your side, or the person who sits in the cubicle next to you. That is why, for so many years, I never told anyone much. I thought it was irrelevant.

❁

In late September 2019, I sat in a sticky, turquoise-colored booth at a fifties-style diner in rural Connecticut with a dear friend. One of the couples who became like family to me in Amsterdam was getting married, and they kindly allowed me to bring a friend as my guest, as I wouldn't know anyone else at the wedding and was as single as they come. I took it as an opportunity to bring one of my closest friends who had met this particular couple when she visited Amsterdam. I had only been back in New York about three weeks at this point, and we were still playing catch-up. We had known of each other since elementary school, but since we went to different primary schools, we really didn't get to know each other well until we were joined up in the same high school in tenth grade. We became fast friends, and our friendship matured as we aged.

Here we sat, in our early thirties, me having just returned from living abroad, and her having just begun her career after years of schooling to obtain her PhD in clinical psychology. In that eatery called "Dotty's" (which also happens to be my maternal grandmother's name), over fluffy eggs and mouthwatering peanut butter chip pancakes, my psychologist friend encouraged me to reconnect with my past. She encouraged me to talk to someone. Yes, she is a professional therapist, but she was also acting as a concerned friend.

I was at a crossroads, both professionally and personally, and I had so much to learn about myself and my happiness. That conversation sent me down the most trying path of self-discovery I had yet to experience—a path I am still venturing on today.

We are shaped by our experiences—both good and bad. That, I know now, is where we each get our unique power. By suppressing the bad, you end up suppressing a lot of what you've learned along the way. And if we cannot learn, we cannot grow.

I was about to learn and grow in ways I never thought possible. And it is my resilience that got me through what could only be described as a completely tumultuous stretch ahead.

Chapter 23

A STORY OF THANKSGIVING

For the rest of Q4 2019, I felt like a cartoon character with a chronic rain cloud over my head. It followed me everywhere I went and stole any bit of joy I could latch onto. At least, that is how I later came to describe it to one therapist.

It was like I had selected a chocolate from the box that had some disgusting jelly filling—my least favorite—and instead of tossing the box aside, I just kept biting into the wrong ones. I couldn't seem to find the caramel.

And then things got . . . worse.

Thanksgiving has always been my favorite holiday. As I shared earlier, it gave me such joy to host those two Thanksgiving celebrations with colleagues during my years in Amsterdam.

One of the reasons why I love Thanksgiving is that it's a time of reflection, of giving thanks. There are no presents involved (except for the chocolate Madeline turkeys my mom gives us all each year). It's about family, and food. What is not to love?

Toward the end of 2019, my mom and I traveled down to the DC area to help my sister host her first Thanksgiving. I was such a pro now, after my hosting spells in Amsterdam. She and her husband and their four-year-old were newly settled in their house, and she invited us, her in-laws, and their extended family to celebrate with them. Seemed like a totally appropriate thing for an almost nine-month pregnant lady to be doing for the first time, right? Especially when she would rather eat Italian than traditional Thanksgiving food, as we're reminded each year. I, on the other hand, absolutely loved cooking for Thanksgiving.

We arrived in Maryland on Tuesday evening. I worked my day job remotely for half of Wednesday, and then it was time to get to the more "crucial" work of chopping, peeling, and sautéing. It was supposed to be a special afternoon—the first time my niece was old enough to help out. There were three generations of Adelman/Schwartz women preparing a Thanksgiving feast together.

As some Broadway soundtrack tolled in the background—likely from *Wicked* or *Hamilton*—I noticed my niece was so connected to my mom. She only wanted to sit on *her* lap, only wanted to help cut *her* pepper or mushroom. As the only contact lens-wearer (finally) in the family, I got stuck solo, on the other side of the table, with the onions. Every time I would ask her a question about pre-school or whatever to try and connect, she barely answered.

How could this have happened? I flew home every year for her birthday. I got her the best European kids' gifts anyone could want—clothes from chic boutiques, Peppa Pig books straight from London, and even Paddington Bear (the stuffed animal *and* book set). She came to visit me in Amsterdam with my sister, and we took her to Disneyland in Paris. We both begged my sister to walk with us to the best ice cream parlor in Paris so we could indulge in chocolate cones on an unseasonably warm March day. We enjoyed our treats in front of Notre Dame one month before the infamous fire. But here I was, less than three feet away, in person, and she was treating me like a virtual stranger.

I was absolutely crushed, and my mood soured.

Thanksgiving rolled around. I felt like I was just there in body only. The day came and went—period.

The day after, we dabbled in some Black Friday shopping—a

ridiculous but special tradition that dates back to my childhood years. My mom, sister, and I would go see a Broadway show the day after Thanksgiving and end it by braving the crowds at "the big Macy's" in Herald Square. Why did we do this? I still do not know. But hey, tradition is tradition, right?

On this trip, I was looking forward to seeing one of my best friends from UNC who lived in DC on the Saturday. I had met her son only once, the previous year on one of my trips back—I was likely in town for my niece's birthday . . .

Early that Saturday morning, I woke up with a raging stomachache. I looked at the clock—6 a.m. As someone who enjoys sleeping in, this was way too early to wake up on a day off.

No stranger to the world of upset stomachs, I figured I had eaten too many leftovers the day before and was being punished accordingly. I willed myself to go back to sleep, which lasted about five minutes.

I made my way upstairs to the bathroom and threw up. Still feeling bad, I crept back downstairs. I kept trying to close my eyes and get comfortable until around 8:15 a.m. Then I deemed it appropriate to crawl into my mom's cozy bed, which was conveniently located upstairs.

She was just getting up and asked, "What's wrong?"

"Nothing. My stomach hurts. I just want to sleep a little longer in a more comfortable bed," I said.

"Ok. I am going to go play with Alani." And she was off.

I dozed in and out, but my breath was growing shallow and the pain was tighter. Between trips to the bathroom and lying there holding my stomach, I was doubled over in pain.

At about 10 a.m., I mustered up enough strength to text my friend to tell her I wasn't feeling well and would keep her posted. I wasn't sure if I would be able to meet her as planned.

Around that time, my mom came in to check on me. I was as pale as a ghost—this was no ordinary stomachache.

My sister suggested we go to urgent care—she made us an appointment. I have no memory of getting into the car; all I know is once I was in there, it was an endless cycle of pain. I couldn't sit, I couldn't lie down. I had a barf bag at the ready.

My mom helped me into the urgent care facility, where I flung myself onto a couch in the waiting area, unable to move. By that point in time, I could no longer open my eyes.

The doctor took one look at me and knew right away: appendicitis. WHAT?!

Well, actually, I don't think I freaked out at that moment. My mom did enough of that for both of us. I was mostly semiconscious and trying not to vomit on this nice doctor.

The doctor told us we needed to go to the emergency room right away in a "Do Not Pass Go. Do Not Collect $200" kind of a way. Before we left, he gave me a strong anti-nausea pill—a gift from God. Within a matter of minutes, I felt alive again. In fact, by the time we reached the hospital, I was convinced I was cured and we'd make it back to NY on our train that evening. Delirium talking.

After hours in a triage room hooked up to an IV, a young doctor finally sent me for an MRI and eventually confirmed what apparently we already knew. My appendix was on the cusp of bursting and needed to be taken out right away.

Within a matter of minutes, I was being introduced to a surgeon and an anesthesiologist. Just before being rolled away, I looked at my mom and asked her to call my sister. I wanted to hear her voice one more time . . . just in case.

By now, you've probably come to realize I can be a tad dramatic. But really, what is a person to think if she's never had surgery before, and has no idea how laparoscopic procedures work? S'pose I should've watched *Grey's Anatomy* like the rest of the world.

I anxiously watched as the anesthesiologist administered the necessary drugs, and the last thing I remember is the oxygen mask being fitted over my face as the florescent lights of the operating room overtook my eyesight and the world went blank.

I woke up, feeling disoriented, in a cold recovery room. The nurse was talking to me a mile a minute. I vaguely remember thinking, *This is probably important information*, but she might as well have been speaking in gibberish. I also remember thinking, *This is silly. Why are you force-feeding me wound-care information when I barely have my eyes open? And where's my mom? Can't you just tell her this info?* Finally, they let my mom into my recovery room. And said nurse had to repeat everything again.

Just as quickly as I came into the hospital, I was out. Seriously. No one could believe they had discharged me the same day. I was in intense pain—different than before, of course. The nurse helped me into the car, and off we went to my sister's house.

Mom stayed by my side for a few days, helping me do the things I couldn't do on my own—like sitting up or going to the bathroom or showering. At some point, I told her she should go back home. She refused to go sans me, but I wasn't able to travel yet. I put on a smile and told her I'd be okay.

For the next few days, my sister and I were a sight—she was plopped down on the couch with me, and in her very pregnant condition, both of us were pretty useless. If the remote fell, we were screwed. That's where my niece came into play. Pretty great having a four-year-old around who would do whatever we said—even for her scary Aunt Day.

My niece, who wanted to be a doctor one day, was fascinated by what happened to me. I told her about it the best way I could: by reading the book Madeline. Madeline, a redhead like me, goes through her own painful experience with appendicitis. We both held her Madeline doll tight as I read the story.

For the rest of my stay, she was the most attentive nurse. She went from wild and rambunctious to calm and tame around me, not wanting to accidentally land hard in my lap and hurt my incisions.

I didn't realize it at the time, but a strong bond was forming between us. One that has only grown stronger over the last two years.

In those few days, while lying helpless on my sister's dark gray leather couch, I found a type of solace that had not been present in a long time.

The solace was temporarily disrupted by the need to fill out my year-end self-evaluation.

One morning, when my brother-in-law was at work, my niece at school, and my sister at a doctor's appointment in DC, I decided I was well enough to sit up and tackle the task. I dragged myself over to the table, fired up my laptop, and stared blankly at the templated form.

I had never had this problem before. The words usually just came to me. I was always able to look at my objectives and document how I had measured up against them, providing strong examples from throughout the year.

This year, however, wasn't like any other. I technically held three different roles, all of them very different. Two of them Amsterdam-based and the most recent role in the US.

Thankfully, before I left the Netherlands, I asked key colleagues for written feedback on my performance. I knew that once I left, it would be hard to get their input for my year-end review, and I really wanted to hear what they had to say—the good stuff and the areas of opportunity.

I started slowly, recapping the first three-quarters of the year. And then I got to September 2019 and froze again. I replayed the last three months in my mind, and before I knew it, I was crying—big, ugly tears that bordered on hysterics. Okay, it was actual hysterics. I sat there, and I did what I had wanted to do for the last few months but was too proud to do: cry.

In my mind, I had messed everything up—my career path, relationships with family. I knew I hadn't been a great friend either.

I knew something needed to change. But what? And how?

And so began an intense period of reflection, even though I didn't realize that right away.

At the time, however, I was focused on one thing: a new meaning for "Thanksgiving." One that came with a newfound appreciation for life, and for being given another chance at it. And a new chance to appreciate my family. Starting there seemed like a good place. The rest would come in due course. It had to.

Chapter 24

FINDING MY VOICE

The appendicitis ordeal took me out for about three weeks. When I returned to work, we were well into December, and the first days were spent at a planning meeting outside the office for the leadership teams who were direct reports of our management team.

It felt nice to be back. Well, really, it felt nice to not be sitting in the same pajamas on my sister's couch watching my cute little niece dance to *Mickey Mouse Clubhouse*.

As the facilitators kicked off, I surveyed the room. I knew almost all the faces, but there were still a few unfamiliar ones I had yet to meet. Either we had never interacted pre-Amsterdam or they had joined the company after I left the NY office. With the exception of two colleagues who were my exact age, I found myself yet again to be the youngest one in the room.

A sense of newfound pride began to form. A sort of "you're back" after being so down. It was refreshing, but I also knew I wasn't magically cured. All those thoughts that were stuck in my head were just that: stuck in my head. I tried to make sense of the situation and muster up the courage to have a real conversation with my boss about how things were going, how I felt, and how I was trying to move forward. Because we were offsite all week, that meeting would have to wait.

One thing was for sure. I was here for a reason. And I was going to participate. I went all in.

❖

A week after the offsite, the opportunity finally came to sit down with my boss. It was a cold, mid-December afternoon. It was pitch dark already, even though it was shortly after lunchtime.

I booked us a conference room upstairs, away from where our team sat. It was the only room available, but it turned out I had selected the one conference room that does not have see-through glass sliding doors and is stationed near HR. It had become to be known as the "room of gloom" because if you're taken in there, well, chances are you aren't coming out happy!

As I led my boss into this room, I think she could tell this was not going to be an ordinary check-in. She asked me how I was feeling—most likely referring to my appendectomy—and that opened the flood gates.

I told her I didn't think this was working and that I was miserable—at work, in life. I told her I was struggling to build relationships with new colleagues. I had always been confident in my opinions, and now everything I seemed to do and say just seemed wrong.

And then, I did what had become par for the course as of late. I started to cry. Big, ugly tears.

I couldn't catch my breath. Come to think of it, I may have been hyperventilating. I was mortified. No—horrified. I had never wailed that hard at work before. Remember, being vulnerable was still something new to me.

Thankfully, she was one of the most empathetic leaders I have ever worked for. She had also been through similar situations, having lived abroad herself and moved back home to her native city. And now, of course, she was abroad again. She was also able to validate my thoughts. Repatriation is tough. There is no rule book for it. Starting a new job—especially in a place that you may think is familiar but has changed significantly—is tough. I wasn't doing as bad of a job as I perceived. I was just adjusting.

That moment did something for me, though. It released so much pent-up emotional energy; so many thoughts that had been floating around solely in my head.

It was the moment I realized I was starting to rediscover my voice.

What does it mean to have a voice? I imagine it means different things to different people. To me, it means being firm in your thoughts and opinions, and being able to express yourself—your wants, needs, and desires—in a productive and professional way. It means guiding others directionally when you can see the big picture, making it simple or tangible for those around you who may not see it. It also means agreeing firmly with others when you concur but equally sharing your view when there's a dissonance. It means being able to admit fault, take responsibility, and own being self-aware.

To refind my voice meant to refind me. My resilience was starting to kick back in, nudging me forward and lifting me up.

I left the office later that evening with my winter coat zipped up tight. The frigid December air was unforgiving, and the walk to the train in the pitch dark could have easily brought me back down. I didn't let it. I couldn't let it. I had come so far, and there was no going back. After all, the air may have been cold, but it was fresh. A new season was upon all of us.

Chapter 25

STEPPING OUT OF THE RAIN

There's a song lyric from the Broadway show, *Dear Evan Hansen*, that gives the listener what seems like obvious advice to step out of the sun if you're getting burned. My "sun" was that previously described raincloud, which, quite honestly, worked better for someone like me with a fair complexion. [Wink.]

How did I finally step out of the raincloud? The answer: see below. *The real answer: I am still working on it.*

I started by booking a two-week trip over Christmas. I wanted to go somewhere familiar, where I had friends and wouldn't totally be alone, but could also retreat and have some alone time. I wanted to go where I knew my way around and felt safe. I didn't want to waste time or energy trying to learn my way around a new place. The thought process sounded exhausting to me, and I was exhausted to begin with. I was essentially left with two options: London or Amsterdam.

I chose both.

I contemplated whether running back to Amsterdam so soon was the answer, but it checked all the boxes. I thought it might be good to finally say goodbye to that life for good, fully close the chapter, and move on. Ten days after I landed, I would be leaving again. It just felt right.

Luckily, two of my good friends (the couple who had recently wed in Connecticut) were going to let me stay in their extra bedroom. I would have about one week with them until they left for their honeymoon, and then one week alone in their place. And keeping with tradition from the last few years, I would join two good friends in London for New Year's. It was the perfect arrangement.

When it came time to board my flight back to Amsterdam, I was filled with a different type of emotion than the melancholic state from my late August return. I didn't have a one-way ticket. This time, there would be a definite departure date. I was excited to go, but also unsure of what I was going to find. Did everything change over the last four months? Would I feel like I belonged, or would I now feel like I didn't belong in either New York City or Amsterdam? Would I find the closure I so desperately craved?

The first few days in Amsterdam, I kept busy. I celebrated the holidays with my two friends. We cooked, we shopped. I met up with old colleagues for drinks. I even went into the office to work remotely for a few days. And then after Christmas, my hosts were off to Bali, and I was on my own. I set a goal to have one plan a day so I wasn't 100 percent alone but left the rest of the days open so I could really rest and recharge—and binge-watch *Game of Thrones* from the beginning. It had always been on my "to-watch" list and I was finally doing it!

In-between episodes, I made lists such as, "What makes me happy"? Answers: cooking, acting, traveling, working out, my job, plan for personal development.

Ok, where would I start?

Cooking? Get back into Whole30 when I get home. January is a great time anyway. Check.

Acting? I could restart acting classes at the studio I used to study at years ago (shoutout to HB Studio in the West Village!). Check.

Traveling? Book the next trip! I knew I was likely going to come back to Europe for my birthday in April 2020. Over my time abroad, we started a tradition—similar to New Year's—because my London friend has her birthday five days after mine. We would pick a location, gather a group of friends, and celebrate in style. In the meantime? I was going out to LA for a day or two in February for work. Could I extend that? Maybe. I could also tack on a few extra days after an upcoming meeting in Orlando in early March 2020. I am not a Disney fanatic, but I do like Disney World. Brings back some of the happier memories from my childhood. Check.

Working out? I could increase my sessions with my trainer. Or try something new? Pilates? Maybe. Check.

What about my job? What could I do at work? I could work with those who I got off to a rocky start with. I am really excited about all the innovations we're working on. I could lean more heavily into that process. It is new and exciting, as I hadn't really supported an innovation agenda before. I am going to put my focus and energy there. Check.

And I was going to update *my* personal development plan. No more of this wandering and putting my career fate in the hands of other people as with the last two years. I needed a clear plan and something to work toward. I needed to have more open conversations with my boss on a more frequent basis. Check.

I knew what I needed to do. Now I just needed to do it.

After a fun thirty-six hours in London for New Year's, and as my trip wound down, I spent my last day catching up with another friend in Amsterdam. We started with a high-intensity interval training (HIIT) workout class. When I went into the class, I had one niece, and when I came out, I was an aunt of two! My sister had gone into labor, and her new daughter was born. I immediately booked a trip to DC to go see her the very next weekend. Another trip booked!

I headed back to the States with a new outlook. You are looking BRIGHT, 2020!

Famous last words.

Chapter 26

THE YOUNGEST ONE IN THE ROOM: COVID-19 TASK FORCE

A piece of advice: if possible, try to plan your comeback well in advance of an emerging global pandemic.

By February 2020, I was in a groove. Life was going well. I started off each week with a Monday evening acting class at HB Studio and successfully completed the Whole30 in January. I got out and started dating, began seeing a therapist, and would be taking on the role of maid of honor for one of my best friend's upcoming April 2020 wedding. (Spoiler alert: the wedding didn't happen in April as planned.)

Work was going well too. We were preparing to launch a slate of new products that would take the company from being a beer company to a beverage company; it was an incredibly exciting time. The innovation team adopted me, and I latched on like a new puppy experiencing their world for the first time. I joined their brand-building workshops for the new products, where we looked at everything from product name to product purpose, and participated in branding exercises for the new innovation arm of the company, where we defined our role, purpose, and values as a company. I also got to bring in my own agency partners to support the communications efforts of the launch. I had settled into my day job and leaned into building a rapport with my direct report.

It was important to me to build my capability as a people leader. I didn't want what was going on in my personal life to impact my ability to grow and develop my teammate. That wouldn't be fair. However, what I didn't realize at the time was that vulnerability is not just about being open with peers and superiors. It very much applies when leading a team. In fact, it might be the most important time to be vulnerable in the workplace. This would be a hard lesson to learn as I leaned into becoming a people leader over the next few months.

My resilience had not failed me before, and at the beginning of 2020, it was pushing me forward for the first time in months.

At the same time, there were rumblings of a new "COVID-19" virus that had popped up in Asia. But that was on the other side of the world.

By mid-to-late February, being that I worked for a global company, HQ in Amsterdam was suggesting that each market prepare a task force. It looked like the worldwide spread of this virus was inevitable. My boss and a colleague in HR—who was always two steps ahead—had already been talking about this. Our first official meeting was scheduled for that last week in February. I remember this vividly because it took place directly following my 2019 performance review (yes, the one I wrote up while recovering from appendicitis on my sister's couch last Thanksgiving). My boss and I would have to finish the review conversation at another time because we had to head upstairs for the task force kickoff.

The initial COVID-19 task force consisted of our chief executive officer, chief sales officer, chief corporate affairs officer (my boss), chief legal counsel, chief of operations, a senior colleague from HR, and myself, a director of communications. Once again, I was the youngest one in the room.

As we sorted through what would eventually need to be done if the virus made its way to the Western world, we were also preparing for our all-employee meeting, which was scheduled to start the following week. We made the decision to move forward with the meeting, with all the facts we had on the table at the time, and based on what the US government was saying. Of course, no one knew the real dangers and threat of COVID-19 less than two months into 2020.

We touched down in Orlando and kept a watchful eye on the news. These were the early days when all we knew was that the virus was reportedly spotted in Italy, and sanitizing your hands was important.

Our meeting started on a Monday and adjourned after the Wednesday evening event. Employees either headed home Thursday or chose to stay a few extra days to enjoy what Orlando had to offer.

After the conference, on Friday, we called another task force meeting. It was becoming clear that we'd have to move into action as we saw Europe—Italy, Spain—begin to fall victim to COVID. It was only a matter of time before it was headed our way.

I remember looking at my boss right after that call. The air conditioner was blasting in the hotel conference room, and it was mercilessly cold. I was nervous, but somehow felt ready for what was to come at the same time. I said, "I think my training in crisis communications is about to become really useful."

What happened next, I can recall in clear, chilling detail.

Friday, March 6: I took what would be my last flight for almost eighteen months home to New York. No real concern of infection, but there was a rising anxiety in all of us passengers, and everyone was keen to get home.

Saturday, March 7: My best friend's bridal shower! Groups of women gathered. There was hugging, close conversations. No masks. No talk of COVID, although I imagine it was subconsciously on everyone's mind. It was to be the last social gathering for a very long time.

Wednesday, March 11: then-President Trump addressed the nation. He announced the first border closure for thirty days, at first announcing this was for both leisure and commercial purposes. Within minutes, we had inquiries from the media asking what this meant for us, an importer in the US from both Europe and Mexico. Would we be able to get products into the country? Turns out he meant to say "only leisure . . ."

Thursday, March 12: then-New York State Governor Andrew Cuomo sent the National Guard to New Rochelle, New York, a village less than two miles from our office. He sent them with the intent of isolating the first known case in New York, which was pegged to a lawyer and resident who had already spread the virus to others in the community. Our task force sat together in the office and made a decision. This is the first and only time the COVID-19 task force would all be in the same room over the course of its existence.

Our sixth email within ten business days went out to all our employees, alerting them that office-based workers should work from home through the end of the month. Along with the rest of the world, we thought we'd evaluate the situation at the end of March 2020. Little did we know back then that the office wouldn't attempt to be reopened—and on a voluntary basis at that—until October 2021. Employees were told to just take what they needed for the expected two to three weeks. We all genuinely thought we'd be back come April.

In addition to taking on the duties of the task force, the business needed help from our team—the corporate affairs team—now more than ever. A newly released campaign for one brand was now considered to be grossly insensitive, given the external climate. Everything needed to be pulled immediately, and media plans with the other brands needed to shift. Summer campaigns that were about to roll out were shelved. My peers in other companies were experiencing comparable madness as well.

As one of only two nonexecutive team members on the task force, all the random inquiries from across the business were coming to us. People wanted guidance on how to operate on all levels, and the word "unprecedented" dominated everyone's vocabulary.

Friday, March 13: Our first official day of working from home—and the first day New York was entering into a state of "emergency lockdown." I was holed up at the desk in my apartment, which was located in my (thankfully) larger-than-normal NYC bedroom. I was grateful I had a proper setup from the get-go and didn't have to work slumped over on the couch, but it certainly still didn't feel natural. I never worked from home unless I was sick (and shouldn't have been working).

While I loved that apartment, my unit was at the back of the building and faced another building. Therefore, it was very dark, even at midday. I relocated all the floor lamps in my apartment around my desk to provide proper light, but it never really did the job of replacing real sunlight.

My desk was positioned parallel to my bed. As I sat in on the daily task force call, a majority of my company's management team could see my bed and Andrew Cuomo's face on my small bedroom TV (blasting CNN programming on a repeating cycle) behind me.

We prepared to send what had become our "daily note" to our US-based employees. The tone was calm yet transparent. We shared what we knew. We reminded employees to remain pragmatic. We made it clear that we were not health experts, but we felt a sense of duty to point everyone to the resources coming from the CDC, the World Health Organization, and local and state health departments. We encouraged individuals to seek medical attention if they exhibited any flu-like symptoms.

The daily email went out early in the afternoon.

A few hours later, on Friday evening, we received a call—one of our colleagues had tested positive for COVID-19 and was in the hospital.

From that moment forward, everything became a blur. We jumped into action. We initiated the daunting task of figuring out how to do contact tracing. We drafted a communication to inform all employees. What tone to strike? We wanted to be informative without causing mass panic. We chose to protect the identity of the colleague while alerting those who may have been in close contact. We noted we were in direct communication with our colleague who had become ill and pointed out that this colleague was in high spirits, and in the care of doctors. The email went out that evening.

Saturday, March 14: I decided to go for a long walk with a friend. We walked from the Upper West Side to the Upper East. At this point, New Yorkers were still going outside, being cautious, but NYC was still in full operation. Stores, restaurants, and shops were still open. No mention of masks or gloves. Just sanitizer, which, along with toilet paper, was already sold out. We walked to Forty Carrots inside Bloomingdale's on Fifty-Ninth Street and treated ourselves to frozen yogurt (inside). My friend, the fiancée, was very worried about her upcoming wedding that had been scheduled, planned, and fully paid for five weeks' time. I felt terrible for her but tried to remain positive. "I'm sure it will be fine by then!"

My phone rang abruptly. It was my boss.

"Are you home?" she asked.

"I'm out with a friend. Is everything ok?" I responded. Nervous of what might come next.

"It's [our colleague]. He's taken a turn and is now in the ICU. We are going to jump on a task force call in thirty minutes. Can you join?"

"Of course. I will jump in a cab now. Be home in fifteen," I replied.

My friend understood the rush to leave in a hurry. I flagged down a yellow taxi and made it home on schedule.

I didn't sit at my desk. I sat at my dining room table. Friday, the day before, had been one official business day of working from home, and I already needed a change of scenery by Saturday.

We dialed in remotely. The news was not good. We learned he had underlying conditions. We still didn't know anything about this virus, but we knew that having underlying conditions was not good.

It was a somber dialogue. No one knew what was coming next for our hospitalized colleague, but the situation was hopeful. Even though it was Saturday, we concluded that it would be necessary to inform our workforce. We shared our colleague's name for the first time because we knew many of them would want to keep him in their thoughts and prayers. It was the right thing to do.

We also determined that it was best for our CEO to do a livestream on Monday morning. This type of update warranted one.

Sunday, March 15: I needed some air. It was unseasonably warm and sunny. I went on a walk with the soon-to-be-newlyweds who lived in my neighborhood. We walked through Central Park cautiously—a little distance between each other instead of the usual close side-by-side. We grabbed a late afternoon bite at a restaurant outdoors. Something eerie was in the air, but none of us knew what we were in for in the coming days.

Monday, March 16: Our CEO in the US presented her first video message via Workplace (by Facebook, now Meta). It was a one-way livestream where employees could leave comments that she would see after she had addressed the company. She showed us her new workspace—the dining room table—and told us all it was okay to have children running around, dogs barking, babies crying. This was our new normal, and no one had to apologize for it.

First and foremost, she offered a moment of silence for our colleague, whose condition had stabilized but was still in the ICU. She checked in to see how our workforce was doing. She implored our colleagues to practice "social distancing," as the phrase that had just entered our vernacular, and asked employees to limit in-person interactions—to do our parts in slowing down the spread.

All of her updates followed the same two priorities in order of importance:

1. Safety first! The health and well-being of our workforce, which was being looked after by the task force.

2. Business continuity. Sub-task forces would be formed to deal with the commercial aspects of the business in real time, while the situation continued to unfold before us in an unprecedented way.

Task force duties aside, agencies were calling off the hook to pitch new, in-the-moment ideas. Business inquiries were rolling in fast and furiously. I was completely overwhelmed but took it upon myself to be a resource for all of it.

To be honest, the non-stop 24/7 pace was exhilarating at first and provided a distraction from what was going on outside my four walls in my own city. Within a matter of days, NYC was proclaimed to be the new epicenter of the virus. The walk I took on Sunday and the meal we shared after would be the last for months to come.

Thursday, March 19: Our beloved colleague passed away.

The shock sent a shiver down my spine. How could this have happened? His condition had stabilized. Things were looking good. I knew him. He was around my age.

We took a moment, as a task force, to absorb the news together, but we had a duty to fulfill. We had to tell our people.

As a professional communicator, I've ghostwritten many documents for executives. The best ones, of course, are the ones that bring good news—great business results, new product launches, a new program for employees. I like to find creative ways to say things. It's one of the reasons why I went into corporate communications instead of journalism. I didn't like sticking to the confounds of the inverted pyramid and focusing on the five W's (who/what/where/when/why). I wanted to use flowery language to paint a real picture and tell a story.

Then there were challenging ones to write—bad business results, an organizational change that might impact people's jobs, or communications centered around an issue or crisis that needed to be relayed in a precise way to internal and external audiences. These were never as easy as the good updates, but I've been conditioned to do them in my sleep.

This was new. This was unwelcomed. *This was someone's life.* How do you suggest talking points? How do you provide guidance? How do you support an executive in doing something that is absolutely heart-wrenching for those delivering the message and those on the receiving end?

There is no easy answer to this. You band together with your colleagues. You do it together.

My boss and I helped create the initial draft for the message to our employees. Our CEO tweaked it and made it her own. It was raw. It was real. It came from her heart.

Shockwaves reverberated through the company. I spoke with many individuals one-on-one. There was no right thing to say, no way to make it better. In that moment, we were all just there for each other, and sometimes that was enough.

Around 4 p.m., I got up out of my desk chair for the first time all day. I left my bedroom and walked into the living room. I sat on the edge of my couch and just stared. My boss called me about twenty minutes later to check in, and for the first time in several days of being the rock for everyone else in the company, the tears came. I cried.

We closed the "office" on Friday, March 20 as a day of remembrance for our colleague. We were only one week into what would become a multi-month global pandemic, but staff members were exhausted. The task force was exhausted.

Monday, the sun would rise again and we'd be back up and running (from our home offices), and if I had learned anything over the previous two weeks, it was that life is precious. It is not to be taken for granted. Each day is a gift.

As a tribute to our fallen colleague, I vowed from that point on to make every single day count. That's what he would have done had he been given the chance.

Chapter 27

A DECADE OF LEARNING

Most New Yorkers have their own terrifying accounts of how March 2020 went in NYC. What was it like outside? Well, it wasn't exactly the desolate picture of a New York frozen in time that was being painted on some news programs. That might have been the case in Midtown—a bleak Times Square void of tourists with the larger-than-life digital video screens reminding people to stay home and social distance, and thanking our healthcare workers and first responders for being on the frontline of this "war."

On the Upper West Side, where I lived, it was definitely quiet. Quieter than usual. At night, I could hear the horns from the Metro-North trains from the Harlem–125th Street station roaring—which was over three miles away. I could also hear helicopters overhead at all hours of the day, likely airlifting patients to open ICU units and the US Navy ship that became a floating hospital in the Hudson River. You could hear people at 7:00 p.m. respectfully clapping for the healthcare workers from their balconies or windows. The stores on Columbus Avenue that I would normally pass every day—coffee shops, flower shops, the cleaners, a deli—were shuttered. All closed. All with their own version of a heartfelt message on the door urging passersby to stay home and do their part in flattening the curve so that one day soon, the stores could reopen. I prayed that would be the case.

After quarantining for several weeks, I finally agreed to let my mom come pick me up and take me to Long Island. She still lived in the house where I grew up. She was alone, and I was alone. At first I thought I'd go for the month of April—it would be nice to celebrate Passover together (via FaceTime with the rest of our family) and to not be alone on my birthday at the end of the month, if "this thing" lasted that long.

She came on a sunny Saturday. It would've been the most perfect early spring day. The air was warmer for the first time, and the first buds of the season were starting to surface. But something was noticeably different. For starters, she had her pick of curb to park against on Eighty-Seventh and Central Park West—a rarity for anyone who has tried to secure a coveted street parking spot in the area.

As she started to get out of the car to help me with my bag, I screamed, "Do not get out of the car!"

I was incredibly worried about her health. She had just undergone a medical procedure, and there were more treatments to come that would lower her immunity. We had to keep her as healthy as possible, and even with no one else in sight, we still knew little about the virus.

I packed up the car with a suitcase, my desk chair, some select spices I needed to keep up my cooking routine at her place—I had started my own nightly cooking "show" to entertain myself and friends shared in small snippets via text message, and a few other odds and ends. We picked up a pizza from Mama's TOO! on Broadway, and we made the journey east in record time. There was absolutely no one on the road.

She worked at the desk in my sister's childhood bedroom during the day, and I worked from her dining room table all hours of the day. I admired her tenacity during these days. Here was a schoolteacher just two years away from retirement, who had never spent a day of her career behind a laptop. She adapted like she was twenty years old, learning new programs and trying to figure out how to command her elementary students' attention while most of them lay in bed or were distracted by

Nickelodeon blaring in the background on TV.

At some point in early May, I had been running on pure adrenaline for several weeks straight, and I was getting to the point of collapse. Technically, it was still early in the pandemic—even though we didn't know it yet. These were the days when people enjoyed virtual happy hours or got creative with internet-driven virtual quizzes and the like with colleagues and friends.

Around this time, I had a plan to catch up with a colleague, just to check in. She worked in the events and activation team for our business, so her whole professional world had really come tumbling down. Always a sympathetic ear, our conversations brought sunshine to my otherwise dreary days. At some point in the conversation, she said to me, "Hang in there. You are working on stuff that careers are made of."

Those words stuck with me for months and months, because I think she was right. As I internalized what she said in the days after our conversation, I couldn't help but think of the date: May 2020. Exactly ten years since I graduated UNC and began working.

I had hit a decade in the workforce, and what a decade it had been! Ten years of adding to my roster of countless Forrest Gump moments in my life.

This moment also brought me into a welcome, upward spiral of reflection. The number of memories that brought smiles to my face were endless. The number of lessons I've learned are numerous. And maybe, most important of all, the amount of growth I've undergone—from the person I was then to the person I am now—is absolutely tremendous.

It was at this moment I came to realize that every success comes with a key lesson. Every failure, mistake, or misstep was an opportunity to learn. I was starting to become okay with the fact that sometimes you take six steps forward and sometimes six steps backward. Sometimes you reach the end of the path. Sure, it can be deflating, defeating, and even depressing. But what I learned is that, in these situations, in order to move forward, I need to figure out what moving forward means to me, and how I get there. Only then can I pick myself up and get back on the road.

I learned that sometimes I will be told I am the best at what I do. I will be recognized for it with promotions and raises. Maybe even awards and speaking opportunities will follow. In these moments, I will never forget to take pride in my accomplishments and pat myself on the back, but more importantly, I will not forget the hard work that got me there.

I know I will continue to be told I'm not ready, or not good enough. Or that I am a terrible writer. I know there will continue to be those people who redo my work for seemingly no reason.

I've learned to recognize when I'm wrong. I am wrong, unfortunately, more than I would like to be. Because I (sometimes!) know when I am wrong, it gives me confidence to not back down when I am actually right.

Even as I grow older and more established in my career, sometimes I will still be the youngest one in the room. The only female. The only American. The only . . . and the list goes on. I know now that I am there for a reason. I need to own it. Live in that moment. And reflect on it after.

I might still be the youngest person in the room, given the situation with the COVID-19 task force, but it holds a different weight and comes with a different meaning than it did during that first experience in June 2010.

In all of this, I've learned that you need to live to *learn*. And I believe now that the real magic in life happens once you really start to learn *how* to learn!

By the end of May 2020, I had put pen to paper and had a new, refreshed personal development plan. I set new goals, new ambitions. I had something clear to work toward again. I knew what types of opportunities I wanted, where I would be willing to go geographically for them, and how I wanted to be stretched and challenged. I felt really good about my plan, even though I knew there might be some short stops or roadblocks along the way. That was okay because my eye was on a new prize. I wanted to be the head of a corporate affairs department. I wanted to sit on a management team. I wanted to stretch myself further than I had stretched myself before. I had direction again, and I was starting to operate from a place of values and purpose.

In May 2020, I found myself tired, stressed, and overwhelmed in the midst of being a small part of leading an organization through a big global pandemic. But I was proud of the spot I earned to get there and the role I got to play. That kept me going for the rollercoaster of a year that was still to come.

Chapter 28

THE ROAD AHEAD

M ay 27, 2021. One year and two months since New York's lockdown
and reign of "COVID-19 terror." At this point in time, we're still
not out of the woods. I was waiting to close on my newly purchased
apartment in NYC. Yet another major milestone I was incredibly proud
to accomplish on my ambitious bucket list. I always dreamed of owning
my little piece of New York, and was now within arm's reach. I would
be putting down roots on the Upper West Side.

It's Sunday morning, around 10:15 a.m. I'm on the road, heading
back to NYC on a cold and rainy Memorial Day weekend. The weather
was a bust, so I decided to get a jump on the holiday traffic. If I can't be
at the beach, then I should be home packing for my move.

Earlier that morning, I had woken up in my childhood bedroom. I
wanted to hit the road around 8:30 a.m., but my mom was still sleeping.
I didn't want to leave without saying goodbye so I puttered around my
room. I opened my high school yearbook for the first time in over a
decade and read the messages people wrote, went through old photos, and
read the news clippings my sister used to create a collage of me playing
Boo Levy in my freshman year at UNC in *The Last Night of Ballyhoo*.

I smiled. I didn't want to take that part. In fact, when I was cast, I was shocked. I was the youngest one in the cast, yet I was playing the oldest matriarch of the family. *This must be wrong. I'm supposed to be the young daughter.*

It was my mom who told me it was meant to be. What a challenge it would be. And what a challenge it was.

I embodied Boo Levy, a lady whom I determined carried the weight of her worries in her lower back, which differed from where I carry my own worries—in my shoulders. A lady whom I determined would speak like Jessica Tandy, whose character was an elderly Jewish woman from Atlanta in the movie *Driving Miss Daisy*.

As a northerner, I watched the movie on repeat so I could study Jessica's speech patterns, her accent, and her every move. How does a southern lady move? What are her mannerisms? Her facial expressions? Where does she carry her worries and woes?

I practiced my lines every night in the study lounge in the Ehringhaus South dorm, usually with my mom half asleep on the other line. As Boo would say, "Bless her heart."

And then, it was showtime.

The cast was magnetic, the energy electric. We had bonded. We were a team. There was no star of this show. It was an ensemble piece, and we delivered. Together.

Each night, I transformed into Boo Levy. I was on autopilot for 120 minutes under the bright lights, paying homage to the Jewish ladies of the South. At the end of each performance, my lower back ached, and all my energy was drained—physically, mentally, emotionally. I gave that part my all.

After one performance, we did a talk back with the audience where we spoke about the period piece, which took place in Atlanta in 1948. A lady in the audience gasped when I answered one of the questions. My southern accent was gone, and she was simply aghast. She came up to me after and told me she was convinced I was a true southerner and that my performance had moved her. She told me that she hoped this was the career path I'd pursue. It's one of those moments I've committed to memory. One of the highlights of my life.

As I sat there on that chilly and wet morning, eleven years after graduation, I couldn't help but wonder, had I chosen the wrong path? Should I have stuck with the PR internship and then taken time to test my luck in the NY theater scene? Am I really doing what I am meant to be doing?

I snapped back to reality and continued the trip down memory lane. I ended my tour with a photo that caught my eye. It was an odd shape, 4 x 5 inches, and old. I picked it up. The plastic slip contained two photos—one of my maternal grandparents walking down the aisle at my parents' wedding in 1981, and on the other side, one of my paternal grandparents.

There was a soft knock on my door. My mom came in. Finally, she was awake!

I asked her why the photo was in my room.

"I found it the other day and just wanted to show you. Look how young, how happy everyone was."

"Can I keep it?" I asked.

"Yeah, I guess. If you want it."

I slipped it into my handbag, kissed her goodbye, and was on my way.

In the car, the radio was on softly. I always check the clock on drives to Manhattan. I like to time how long it takes, especially since there are fewer cars on the road these days. 10:05. 10:10. 10:15.

The rain is coming down. It's soft but blinding at the same time. I'm going about 60 mph. The speed limit is 55 mph.

I'm in the left lane on the Long Island Expressway and traffic is moving. And then it feels like the steering wheel is locked. The car starts to veer to the left into the HOV lane. What the f*ck. I try to regain control. I can't. There is no control.

Before I know it, the car has thrust itself in the other direction. It feels like my neck has snapped, and I'm gliding across all four lanes of traffic. The seatbelt is digging into my neck, but that's the least of my worries. Because not only am I spinning out of control in the middle of traffic, now I'm going full speed ahead into the shoulder, which is narrow and cut off due to a concrete construction roadblock.

These are those moments. The ones where people say you see your life flash before your eyes. A young, gregarious child. A well-rounded teen. My first kiss in the woods at summer camp. Scoring a goal in soccer. The adrenaline felt on a stage during *Pippin*, that first show at the local theater that became my second home during my teen years. Life of the party in college. Interning in London. Traveling the world. A daughter, a sister, a granddaughter, a friend, an aunt.

Have I done what I've come to do? Have I lived the life I've wanted to live?

WAIT! I'm not done. I'm not through. Not today. This is NOT how my story ends.

I slam on the break with all my might, hoping it will work, so I can regain control of the vehicle. This happens just as the nose of the car meets the concrete barrier. The impact sends a jolt through the car—from the right to the left. My neck follows suit.

It stops. I quickly put the car in park, set the parking break, and shut off the ignition. I shake. I can barely breathe. My mouth opens but there is no sound. My lip is quivering. My head is buzzing. Am I alive? I do not know.

I must be. I didn't crash. I don't think? To the naked eye, it looks like I've completed the perfect parallel park on a very narrow shoulder.

The cars zip by; the rain falls. I snap back to reality.

How come no one stopped to help me? Oh wait, anyone who saw was likely trying to swerve out of the way so I didn't hit them as I cruised across all lanes of traffic.

My neck hurts. As does my head.

I need to call for help. I should call my mom. But she's going to be so worried. I sit a little longer. Absolutely stunned.

I reach into my bag.

Is the car going to explode? What the hell just happened? Should I get out? But where would I go? The shoulder is too narrow. I would get hit and it is raining.

My hands are shaking. My heart, racing. My neck hurts like HELL.

My hand lands on an unfamiliar item in my bag. It's not my phone, but I pull it out. It's the photo of my grandparents. They're smiling at me.

The tears finally come. I cry, no—I am wailing. I know I'm still alive. I find my phone and dial "HOME."

My mom answers. I've stopped crying, but I'm in shock. Utter shock. All I can get out is, "I'm okay. Don't worry, I'm okay." Over and over.

Clearly, not okay.

"Where are you?" she asks.

"I . . . I . . ."

I have no idea. I guesstimate.

"Somewhere between [there and here]. Just come. Drive slow. I'm on the side of the road. You'll see me."

She gets dressed, and she and her boyfriend come to get me. I slide into the passenger seat while I wait. I don't want to be behind the wheel anymore. I still shake. My mouth is dry. My head aches; my neck does too. I stare straight ahead. My neck won't let me do much else anyway.

Her car pulls up. I run in. We hug. I cry. I try to explain, but I just don't know.

She offers me water. "Do you also want something to eat?" she asks.

"*To eat?*" I say, utterly confused.

I spot the snack bag she's managed to pack since I called, just in case I was hungry. A Jewish mother if I've ever seen one!

"I threw in clementines, pretzels, garlic knots from last night's dinner, a Hershey's Kiss—"

Garlic knots?!

I opt for a Hershey's Kiss. I need the sugar.

The tow truck comes. The police never show.

"What happened," he asks?

I do not know.

We dutifully follow after my car is loaded up and dragged away.

We stop at a nearby automobile repair facility, but it's closed. Sunday on a holiday weekend. We leave it parked there, and we go back to my mom's. I sleep for what seems like forever.

Due to the holiday, it would take two days to find out what happened. The mechanic called to tell me it was a freak accident: the part that connects the back wheels to the steering wheel became dislodged and dislocated. I really had no control of the car. I also had two flat tires, but we don't know if that was due to the impact of what happened, or if it contributed to the cause. We'll never know.

Part of me was relieved. Okay, so it wasn't me. I didn't do anything wrong. I didn't black out. *I* didn't lose control.

And the other part of me was horrified. What? This can happen? I'm a city girl. Driving and cars are not my thing.

The road to physical and mental recovery was to be a long one. Five months after the accident, I would still wake up in sweat, thinking about *what if.* Even though the x-rays show I am making progress in my recovery, my sessions at the chiropractor three times a week plus the pain that radiates between the base of the head and my shoulders doesn't let me forget, nor does my lower back.

Now, every day that I wake up and get to put two feet on the ground, I realize, is a gift. I know this now. I like to think I had some guardian angels protecting me that day. Four, to be exact. Even the two who fell out of my life when I was fourteen. And perhaps even my dad who passed in July 2020, at the height of the COVID-19 wave, in Atlanta, where he was living at the time.

When I think about the whole experience—in what couldn't have been longer than sixty seconds in its entirety—I'm still trying to make sense of it. How did I not crash? How was I not hit by another car, or how did I not cruise into another car? I know there were cars in front of me. In the seconds before it happened, I hadn't glanced in the rearview mirror, so I have no memory of what the traffic looked like behind me. It was a busy holiday weekend; there had to be traffic behind me.

After much thought and reflection, here's what I surmise: Life really is like a box of chocolates. You *never* do know what you're going to get.

For me, there is still so much road ahead. Sometimes I'll be cruising easily and carefree, and sometimes I'll be hanging on for dear life. Sometimes there will be pain. Physical. Mental. Emotional. But there will also be lots of joy. Happiness. Fulfillment. Pleasure.

The days of being the youngest one in the room are closing in, but I'm ready for the next chapter. Whatever obstacles lie ahead. I know this now.

ACKNOWLEDGMENTS

I always wanted to write a book. Make that books. Years ago, I came up with the title, *The Youngest One in the Room,* inspired by the client encounter on day two of my professional career, as recounted in this book, and all the instances that would follow. Over the years, as I would be reminded of a memory that I thought would go well in "the book," I'd jot it down. Scraps of paper and notes entered on multiple iPhones accumulated, but I never thought I'd have the guts to tell my own story. And if I did, I never thought it would become my first book. I always pictured myself as more of a historical fiction kind of a gal.

Sometime between Christmas and New Year's in 2020, I was introduced to the very talented career and transition coach, Gia Storm. Once again, at a crossroads in my life at the end of 2020, I needed an impartial voice to talk to about both my career and personal aspirations, and where to go next. The year 2020, of course, was a difficult year for all. I was still very much in a place of evolution after my move back from Amsterdam, tapped out, and dealing with some personal matters that included some health concerns with my mother in early 2020 and the death of my father in July 2020. Oh yeah, there was also a global pandemic going on.

Enter Gia: In one of our very first sessions, Gia gave me a gift—the gift of reflection. Each conversation started with what I had learned since we last left off. It was something no one else had ever given, and it came at a time when I needed it the most.

Within a matter of weeks, that itch I'd had for years to sit down and write was about to be scratched. *Hard.* I decided to shut down the work laptop and open up my own at the end of January 2021 as I settled into a mountain-view room for a week at the Mohonk Mountain House in New Paltz, New York. My mornings were filled with snowshoe walks and mountaintop runs, and my afternoons with writing, fresh-baked cookies, and several cups of hot tea as I watched a fresh layer of snow hit the ground from my cozy abode. And thus, *The Youngest One in the Room* was born.

Would there be a book without Gia? Maybe. Would it have been told from the perspective of capturing a decade of learnings? Most likely not. So, a big, big thank you to Gia Storm for everything you gave me.

I told very few people I was writing a book until the first draft was almost complete. During the trip to Mohonk, I wrote furiously. My outline and a good third of the book were written there. I shared the initial chapters with my biggest fan, my mom. She loved it. I had her laughing and crying. But then she said, "This is great; you know I love your writing, but is there a market for this? Who would read this?"

I knew exactly what she meant. And I agreed with her, but I kept going. This project was becoming more therapeutic than anything else, and once I started, there was no way I was going to stop. This was ultimately for me, and if it never saw the light of day, so be it.

I would take off a Friday here and there and dedicate those days to writing. Given that COVID-19 was still a threat in NYC in those winter and early spring days of 2021, my writing days gave me the escape I so desperately needed from the four walls of my NYC apartment and the monotony of work.

Eventually, I told my boss at the time, who is also a mentor and friend, Josephine Bertrams, about my pet project. She was incredibly supportive, and it meant a lot to have her in my corner during this time. However, too self-conscious, I didn't share the first few chapters with her until September 2021.

Around that time, I reconnected with a friend who I had met while traveling on the Birthright Israel program in 2014. Whitney Holtzman had just published her own book, *You Are the First You*, outlining her incredible career journey, and I was in awe of her ability to publish her story. I reached out, and as luck would have it, she had plans to come to New York at the end of August 2021. We met at one of our favorite spots—*yes,* Forty Carrots in Bloomingdale's Fifty-Ninth Street—for tuna salads and frozen yogurt. We caught each other up on life since we had last seen one another when she visited me in Amsterdam. She also told me the story of how her book came to be.

A few days later, Whitney, the most professional networker I know, had connected me with her publisher. Here I was. I was doing this. I was putting my work out there for judgment. I took a deep breath.

While holding my breath, on the way back from our first annual sister spa outing in September 2021, I told my sister about the book and read her a few chapters as she drove through the Virginia countryside. A rock star mom of two at the time, who had recently rejoined the workforce after a five-year absence to raise her kids, she was glued to every word. She told me there was a lot of relevance in my stories for her. I was shocked. I thought, if there is any audience at all out there for something like this, surely it is just those entering the workforce. This gave me the confidence to keep going.

I started to tell more close family and friends about this venture over time. Simply put, I would tell them, "I am writing a book." I don't say things I don't mean, so by saying this out loud, I was choosing to make it real. The reactions amongst friends were of genuine excitement, but when they asked what genre it was, each time I had to respond, I uncomfortably mumbled, "a memoir?" I still wasn't there yet.

Throughout the fall of 2021, I worked with my team to bring a longtime vision to life at work: launching our first ever corporate communications campaign for the company in the US. Not only did we do that, but it also focused on gender diversity in the alcohol beverage industry, a subject near and dear to my heart. Over Q3 and Q4, we conducted several media interviews with our CEO, Maggie Timoney. Interview after interview, I kept finding myself moved by Maggie's inspiring story. Listening to her speak about her own career journey and what her hopes and dreams were for the next generation of young female talent gave me further confidence to continue writing.

Throughout the course of my writing journey, my mom remained there every step of the way. Always my biggest supporter, she dove into each chapter as I shared and provided her own take on editing ("You missed a comma here"). I am endlessly grateful for the unwavering support she continues to give as she stands behind every step I take in my "create-your-own-Forrest-Gump life adventure."

I finished the first complete draft of the book in November 2021 in the tropical rainforest of Manuel Antonio National Park in Quepos, Costa Rica. Costa Rica had always been high on my list. The pandemic prevented me from getting there as originally planned after my move back from Europe. I wanted four things out of this trip: rest and relaxation, wildlife spotting (e.g., monkeys and sloths), time to read, and time to write. And that I got.

It would take another five months to commit to publishing the book, and then another year of editing while I went on more work and personal adventures. The second draft of the book was completed in Amsterdam at the end of 2022. During 2023, subsequent editing took place in Jakarta, Bali, and Nusa Penida, Indonesia at the same time I achieved my next career stop—a goal I set back in May 2020. I wanted to become the head of corporate affairs for one of the operating companies in my organization. Even more than my gratitude for being able to finalize the editing in some of the most jaw-dropping locations on earth, I am grateful for the opportunity to have led an incredible team and gain my first C-Suite experience as part of the management team and the board of directors.

Throughout this period, the words "I'm writing a book" progressed from a timid mumble to a proud update. I am endlessly grateful for my family and lifelong friends who supported this endeavor and continuously checked in on its progress along the way.

I am also eternally thankful for the friendships I've made over the years from work. I would be remiss not to mention four incredibly special ladies who have not only served as mentors and peers, but more fondly, forever friends: Tara Rush Tripp, Rachel Shell, Kristen Commander, and Carolyn Bos. We may not get to see and speak to each other every day anymore—we may not even get to catch up often—but knowing I always have you four in my corner is one of the greatest gifts "work" has given me.

Lastly, it takes a village to write a book. While the writing is mine and mine alone, I am blessed to have worked with an all-star team of editors and advisors at Indigo River who have guided and challenged me to dig deep every step of the way. Big thank you in particular to Deborah Froese, Marci Carson, Jennie Seitz, and River Chau.

My intent with the book is not, and never will be, to preach. These are my stories and my lessons. This is what I learned on the first part of my professional journey. I do not want to tell others what to do or how to live their lives. As I started writing, I did feel compelled to put it on paper in the hopes that maybe, just maybe, something I said or a lesson I learned could inspire others who may be experiencing the same things.

I have no idea if this book will succeed or fail. I have no idea whether this book will disadvantage me when it comes to potential career opportunities down the road. What I do know is that by putting it out there, I am relinquishing it from my clutches, and instead handing it over to you, the reader, to judge.

I'd like to hear from you and listen to your stories. Please write to me at TheYoungestOneBook@gmail.com. Thank you for coming along on my journey.

ABOUT THE AUTHOR

Dayna Adelman is brewed with a passion for storytelling, the thrill of a travel adventure, and the love of a good challenge. Driven to do things outside the box, she has taken a more unconventional path to finding personal and professional success. That is, if convention is defined by the New York community in which she grew up.

Her career as a corporate affairs professional has taken her to live in four countries on three continents, where, in her first decade, she continued to defy the odds as the youngest—and sometimes only female—in the room.

Dayna is a proud graduate of the University of North Carolina at Chapel Hill with degrees in journalism and dramatic art. Go Tar Heels! Her greatest love is her family. Dayna feels a deep sense of gratitude for her wonderful mother, immense respect and admiration for her sister, and endless amounts of adoration for her three nieces.

She currently resides in New York City.

www.ingramcontent.com/pod-product-compliance
Lightning Source LLC
Chambersburg PA
CBHW070347090426
42733CB00009B/1325